*Entertainn   e areas of
media pr   ournalist,
Ben Falk   the arts
industries   . This is
coupled   d young
profession   urnalism.
Interview   editors of
the bigge   consumer
publicists.   makers,
TV prese

Topics

- break
- inter
- work
- work
- sellin
- using
- break

With   writing
and repo   tainment
world, th   ournalist.

Ben Falk   UK, and
a freelance entertainment journalist. The author of celebrity biographies *Robert Downey Jr: The Fall and Rise of the Comeback Kid* and *The Wonder of Brian Cox*, he has written about showbiz for 20 years, contributing to dozens of magazines, newspapers and websites, including Yahoo Movies, BAFTA, *Look*, and BBC Films Online. He was Hollywood bureau chief for the Press Association and has worked as an entertainment television producer for ITV, Channel 4 and Sky.

ENTERTAINMENT JOURNALISM

Making it your Career

Ben Falk

Routledge
Taylor & Francis Group

LONDON AND NEW YORK

First published 2018
by Routledge
2 Park Square, Milton Park, Abingdon, Oxon OX14 4RN

and by Routledge
711 Third Avenue, New York, NY 10017

Routledge is an imprint of the Taylor & Francis Group, an informa business

British Library Cataloguing-in-Publication Data
A catalogue record for this book is available from the British Library

Library of Congress Cataloging-in-Publication Data
A catalog record for this book has been requested

ISBN: 978-1-138-64937-8 (hbk)
ISBN: 978-1-138-64938-5 (pbk)
ISBN: 978-1-315-62585-0 (ebk)

Typeset in Bembo
by Taylor & Francis Books

CONTENTS

ACKNOWLEDGEMENTS

Obviously, this book wouldn't have been written without the generosity and expertise of friends and colleagues who contributed their advice, so for that, thank you: Colin Paterson, Andy Welch, Alex Stanger, Ben Robinson, Chris Smith, David Smyth, Hannah Hargrave, Jill Foster, Joel Rapaport, Julia White Cohen, Lucy Preacher, Mel Bromley, Natasha Bird, Nikki Cain, Orlando Parfitt, Rosie Nixon, Sophia Moir, Sophie Vokes Dudgeon, Suzy Cox, Tim Muffett, Toby Earle, Tom Butler, Victoria Hollingsworth, Lisa Perry and Zak Brilliant.

Thank you to Jane Crowther for loan of her narrative skills and to Mum, Dad, Christina, Hannah and Marnie for putting up with me while I wrote this thing. Pops, obviously I wouldn't have even got into this racket if it wasn't for you.

Thanks to Kitty, Margaret and Niall at Routledge, Maggie for copy-editing, and my brilliant colleagues at Coventry University and London Met for helping me hone my teaching chops, some of which I've hopefully disseminated here.

And finally to every commissioning editor or boss who's ever hired me – thank you, and if you can keep doing it, that would be awesome …

INTRODUCTION

This is not a textbook. I mean it is, kind of, in that it's published by an academic publisher and you're likely reading it having got it out of a library or from the reference section of your local bookshop.

No, I prefer to call this a how-to guide. A training manual really – aimed at helping you become a working, successful journalist in the world of arts and showbiz. It's a fun world, and while tough and requiring hard work, it's a world you can make your living in. Do it well and it also means you get to indulge your hobby as a job. And before anyone tells you that popular culture is trivial and meaningless, consider this. Donald Trump was part of popular culture before he became president. The entertainment sphere is worth billions around the globe, and it involves deals which shape governmental policy. The depictions in movies and the actions of celebrities and the like help people decide what to wear and how to act as well as being barometers of social equality, arbiters of change and predictors of technological shifts. Entertainment can be a short news story about a structured reality show which you read while you wait for the dentist. It can also matter ... very deeply.

So how am I planning to help you?

There needs to be some background, which is why there's a chapter about the history (or some of it anyway) of entertainment journalism. That may sound academic to you, but knowing how we got to where we are will make you a better journalist now. It's also vital that we consider our place as media creators in a post-Leveson world. While the 2012 report into journalistic behaviour didn't facilitate the kind of seismic change some thought it would, there has nevertheless been a fundamental shift in newsroom attitudes, especially in terms of entertainment reporting.

You're going to hear from experts. As an aspiring journalist, the best thing you can do is learn from people who are already in the industry. "Why?" you may ask. "They're all dinosaurs, social media's changed everything, and the job I'll get probably hasn't even been created yet." Those two latter things may be true – maybe even the first one if you mean they are either a fearsome predator who never gets messed with or a tranquil though even less destructible creature who goes about their business with an unflappable rigour. But remember this: they will likely be the ones deciding whether you are right for the job and letting you cash that pay cheque. They will be the mentors at whose feet you figure out what makes a good story or whether that sentence or sequence you've created is up to snuff compared to the hundreds of successful ones they've outputted. And they will be the ones you look to for information when Google isn't proving to be the information panacea you need it to be.

You will find expert advice dotted throughout this book from current editors of the biggest entertainment brands, Hollywood bureau chiefs and critics, consumer publicists, multimedia content producers, live radio correspondents, video makers, TV presenters and social media specialists. They bring with them decades of collective wisdom as well as up-to-the-minute knowledge on the minutiae of working in this industry. You'd do well to listen.

What will you learn? I hope that this won't be just another book on the shelf about journalism. Of course there are universal skills that pretty much every 'hack' (the word has been reclaimed – I don't mean it pejoratively) needs. Finding scoops, interviewing, using social media and improving your 360-degree multiplatform skills are all things I will discuss. Here, however, they'll be aligned specifically with how they're required as an entertainment and/or arts journalist. There are also elements of craft which are unique to certain facets of this particular type of journalism: reviewing, relationships with PR people and the showbiz diary, conduct on the red carpet and at press junkets, talking to people who are in the public eye and have been interviewed hundreds of times before by an array of often idiotic and unprofessional colleagues. In a time of flux, we'll also cover ways to break into the industry, the notion of personal brand, and selling entertainment material as a freelance.

Your guide through this journey is me. Who am I? Well, I've spent 20 years as an entertainment journalist (I was the aforementioned LA bureau chief for the Press Association), I've been an assistant news editor at *Look*, a writer of consumer and branded content for Yahoo Movies, BAFTA, BBC Films Online, contributor to *Empire, Total Film, Reveal, OK!* and an entertainment producer for Channel 4, ITV, Channel 5 and Sky. There have also been a few books, including biographies of Robert Downey Jr and Professor Brian Cox. There's more, but it's already sounding very self-aggrandising. Now I mix freelance work with teaching journalism at Coventry University.

I only tell you this because I think it's important you know the information contained here comes from a place of experience rather than this being an easy chance for me to enhance my CV by knocking out a book on something I don't really know about. I've lived this job for two decades; it's in my bones and at its best – even at its middling – it's fantastic. It also means I will throw in a few anecdotes and drop a few names. I apologise in advance if they clang too loudly when they hit the ground – there will always be a learning point attached so you don't have to make the same mistake, or at least you can make the same mistake but you'll be a bit more self-aware about it than I was.

I should add that because of my experience and also because of where this book is likely to end up, it'll tend to reference UK and US entertainment. I hope that those of you who are kind enough to pick it up outside of these countries might still find plenty of useful material contained herein. But I'm sorry if there's a lot of mentions of American blockbusters and not all that much about French farce.

1

GETTING AND BREAKING STORIES

If you're going to be a successful entertainment journalist, then you have to be able to break stories. Now this is where a lot of aspiring journalists start to panic. I know – I've seen it. "I'm a nobody; how am I supposed to find a story that no one else has?" "Where does one even start?"

The thing is, for an entertainment journalist, breaking a story doesn't *necessarily* mean what it might if you're a general news reporter working in the front section of a newspaper. It can of course. When I was Assistant News Editor at *Look* magazine, we were constantly approached by news agencies, as well as regular freelance contributors who said they had a story about Angelina Jolie or Jennifer Aniston. A marriage hiccup, a weight issue – typical showbiz tabloid fodder (we'll leave the ethics of this out for the time being, though this will be addressed in Chapter 9). Sometimes, we'd run the story; sometimes we wouldn't. Occasionally, we'd ask the freelancer if they had anything else about a celebrity we particularly wanted to feature that week, and they'd go away and dig around.

Angle

Before you proceed any further with a story, think about whether you have a good angle. If the story is new, what's your take on it? If it's ongoing, what new thing are you bringing to it to move the story forward? If it's a more in-depth piece, why should someone be reading your 1000-word analysis rather than another journalist's? I often tell students to ask themselves the question: why should *you* write about this *now*? Often this causes useful contemplation. Just 'wanting to write about it' normally isn't enough. Unless you're a big-time columnist with carte blanche from your editors and a loyal audience who hang on your every word (and that is a tiny minority of hacks).

Generally, it's not just coming up with a story idea. It's coming up with the angle as well. If you can't do that, then you're really only covering a 'topic'. Good journalists need to be able to see and grasp the key nugget in a topic which will illuminate that topic for an audience.

This is harder than you think. It will come very naturally to some people. Others might take longer, but it's something that – although idiotic naysayers who mostly still wish that a newspaper was written in the pub argue otherwise – can be learned. Through practice. Doing it over and over again. Reading, watching, listening and analysing other people who do it really well and understanding *how* they do. Even, if you're lucky enough, talking to them in person or getting guidance from them about how you can improve and then actually acting on their feedback without grumbling about them constructively criticising you. It's unlikely to be something that you ever truly master, and even if you work in the business for some time, you'll still have plenty of bad days. But don't worry. Never giving up on trying to improve this aspect of your skills will only improve you as a journalist.

Contacts

Contacts are the holy grail for any journalist. It might be that you know someone working inside the White House who's prepared to give you things off the record. It might be that there's a government policy wonk in Whitehall who leaks material or even a boot man at Manchester United who doesn't like the new manager all that much. For the most part, these kinds of contacts are cultivated over a period of time. People are specifically hired by an outlet because of their contact book. And this is where young journalists get panicky – they don't have ten years in the field to build up that kind of relationship, so how are they going to compete?

The thing is, there's a new type of contacts book now, and it's called social media. Social media is such a broad and complex web of communications and relationships that it's a gold mine for any young journalist looking to make their way. My students often complain (and sometimes with good reason) that they find it difficult to get interviewees for their stories. But it's all about lateral thinking. While you *can* approach someone famous on Twitter, and sometimes get a reply, as long as you put in the groundwork, there is a good chance you'll be able to use this platform or something similar, like Instagram, to find someone who knows someone who knows someone. This is often where your contacts book begins. It's unlikely that you're going to be getting quotes from Brad Pitt's best mate straight away. But chatting to someone who knows that guy on the Channel 4 structured reality show? That's a start. And that's what I mean by the entertainment journalist not having to compete in the same way as a hack in the news section for *The Guardian*. The news you'll be covering will be interesting and important to a large swathe of the population, but the stakes are, essentially, lower.

What's more, what constitutes a story in the world of entertainment is vastly different to most other spheres of journalism. The semantics surrounding the word 'news' is something I constantly battle with, and this is particularly the case in showbiz journalism. You wouldn't naturally think a review of a new band's album is a news story, but it is if barely anyone's written about it before. Similarly, the first review of an amazing new movie (or a truly awful one) from a festival could be counted as news within entertainment. This isn't saying that breaking a story about a celebrity marriage break-up or a famous death isn't a great thing to do. But I'd argue that in the entertainment world, both types of story hold the same value. That's not the case, I don't think, in so-called hard news.

So you can start small and begin with some serious digging on social media.

Remember too that cultivating contacts, especially in the entertainment industry, takes time. Did you immediately become close with everyone in your friendship circle? Did you trust your boyfriend enough to reveal everything about yourself to him after the first date? Highly unlikely. But a few weeks or months down the line? Perhaps. Often contacts or sources are part of a long game. They're people you bump into at every red carpet and share a little bit of conversation with you each time. They're the yoga instructor you take classes with for ages before he or she eventually confides in you that one of the ex-One Direction boys is a close personal friend. They're the publicist who you get stuck with at a rubbish launch party and with whom you bond over stale ham sandwiches and warm white wine.

It's always worth being told that a source isn't necessarily someone you would think of immediately. I knew a tabloid journalist who got great gossip out of Brangelina's bodyguard. That's straightforward. But what you can't account for is the random meetings, the accidental contacts you make. And a good journalist always seems to be the one in those places. A good journalist makes their own luck. They think clinically about where they need to be or how they need to stand. They make careful strategic decisions about who to approach and undergo research about how to do it most effectively. I remember seeing long-standing *Daily Mail* correspondent Baz Bamingboye on the Oscars red carpet, standing a long way down the press line. And believe me, there are hundreds of reporters at the Academy Awards, all queuing up to talk to the attendees. He is an established journalist and had covered the ceremony for many years; I couldn't understand why he was prepared to let 50, maybe 70, crews stand in front of him. But then the stars started arriving, and I realised what he was doing. He'd positioned himself on the corner of a barrier facing the arriving stars so that rather than being anonymous amongst the press herd until an actor was literally standing in front of him, they could see him ahead as they walked down the carpet. When they finished the interview before his and looked where to go next, they could see his beaming face right in front of them. Putting himself on a corner also meant that he was able to turn his interviewees away from the rest of the press pack. On the red carpet, it's almost impossible to get an exclusive interview because everyone's standing next to each other. Not so Baz. He carefully turned Rachel Weisz or whoever it was towards him, and no one could hear what she was saying to him. A night of constant exclusive quotes – genius. What's even more infuriating is that I had scoped the area out earlier and decided it wouldn't work for me. Big mistake.

A lot of good reporting is about putting yourself out there, talking to people, insinuating yourself into situations and conversations. But just like any craft – and journalism is a craft despite what its detractors might say – there needs to be background thinking. Some of the best material you'll ever get will be something you fell into at random, sure. But rarely. Most of the best originally reported stories come about through sheer bloody-minded hard work and a lot of nous. Never be afraid of the former or forget the latter.

SOPHIE VOKES-DUDGEON – ONLINE EDITOR, *HELLO!*

What would you say to a person looking to break into your profession right now?

> It's a hard industry to break into, but if you keep knocking, the door will open. When you're given an opportunity, make sure you shine. If work experience is available, be the person who is willing, excited, eager and professional. Be nervous, but do it anyway. And make sure that for every opportunity that ends (a work experience placement, for example), you take away a lead to the next.
>
> Ask people whose jobs you aspire to having if they can spare time for a coffee. Pick their brains; get ideas for what to try next.

What are the three most important things you need as a showbiz reporter?

1. Genuine interest in people. Don't go to an interview with a list of questions and work your way through them. Listen. Have a proper conversation. Share things, talk back, engage your interview subject. They will give you much more interesting answers.
2. News sense. Understand what a story is. With interviews, keep talking until you have discovered something you find interesting. Make sure it's something you would genuinely tell a friend/family member/stranger.
3. Nosiness. It might sound general, but you really can't be a reporter in general if you're not curious. And for celebrity reporting, you need a genuinely nosey nature to come up with the ideas for stories that people will want to read.

How do you see the future of your profession and what might a young person need to know moving forward?

> The landscape of celeb news has changed hugely with the advent of social media. Keeping up with all aspects of social and digital reporting is pretty key I think.

What's the best thing about your job?

There are times most weeks when you really can't believe you're being paid to do this. Each day is different and the subject matter is fun. And you've always got good dinner stories about the time you made Angelina Jolie cry or the time you met Tom Cruise on the red carpet. And although the subject matter is frivolous, the skills that go into investigating and reporting are common to all types of news.

It's also a wonderfully flexible job.

Tell us about your favourite moment/s in your job?

I remember when I started out, screenings and interviews were very exciting. Watching forthcoming episodes of your favourite TV shows then talking to the actors would be fun even if it wasn't your job.

But as I get older I enjoy the challenge of trying to do something better, quicker, from a more interesting angle than your competitors. I've been in a room so jam-packed with stars it feels like a celebrity zoo – Jennifer Aniston dancing next to me, Uma Thurman and Mick Jagger on the far side of the room. Justin Timberlake on the sofa. It feels surreal and fun.

But getting a lead on an exclusive story is a feeling that really makes this job exciting. Like the time I discovered Angelina Jolie's trip to Ethiopia was not just a charity mission but was to adopt a new child. With a lot of publications spending a lot of money trying to make sure these exclusives are theirs, it's a thrill to get an exclusive story.

(Interview with author, 2017)

Reactive/feature pieces

Of course there is breaking news in entertainment journalism, but a large part of the industry is made up of creating feature content. The Pulitzer Prize committee describes feature writing as "non-hard-news stories distinguished by quality of writing. Stories should be memorable for reporting, crafting and creativity". In reality, what constitutes a feature in a modern media landscape is a little broader. For me, that means anything from a long-form, reported article through listicles and reviews to a podcast or documentary. They are all, I believe, a form of feature piece.

A lot, if not the majority, of these will have a newsy hook. They'll be tied to a story of the day or something that's happened during the week. That could be anything from a top ten dig into a musician's oeuvre just after he's died to the profile of an actress who's in a new movie or an audio documentary celebrating the anniversary of the cancellation of a well-loved television show. And for story-finding, this is where it gets important. You need to think plentifully and laterally. You need to find an (if possible) original take. That can prove difficult with entertainment stories. I've sat in countless brainstorming meetings while the participants sit around glumly trying to come up with a fresh feature idea for Christmas or about the Star Wars saga. These have been done to death. So how do you make them different?

Perhaps it's easier if I explain how we came up with our feature ideas at Yahoo Movies UK. We'd have a weekly planning meeting where I'd sit with my editor and his deputy to hammer out some possibilities that they could commission me and the other freelancers to do during the month. We'd start by going through the film release schedule. What's coming out? Who stars in it? What's the premise of the movie? Is it related to other films in some way? We might already have interviews with the on-screen talent lined up, but aside from them, we were looking for clever, interesting and funny ideas which would pull people to the site. A lot of this is Google-related. If something is in the news, people Google it. You want potential reading material to come up on the Google search when they type in "Fast and Furious 462" or "the new Star Trek". So ...

Let's take a movie like *Kong: Skull Island*, which is one that we did brainstorm together.

Ten things ...

You could start with a very simple online listicle feature like "Ten things you never knew about King Kong". While it's not the most scintillating idea in the world, articles like this generate good traffic online because they're easy to digest and you can test your knowledge as a fan against them (most of the time when I wrote these, the comments were filled with irate cinephiles whinging about how they already knew *everything* I'd just written).

Tom Hiddleston

British actor Tom Hiddleston (best known for playing Loki in the Marvel Cinematic Universe) stars in *Skull Island*, so you could write something more specific to him. "Why *Skull Island* proves Tom should be the next Bond", or "How Tom Hiddleston got in shape for *Skull Island*". These kinds of stories pull the focus of the feature a little wider and appeal to the fan base of the actor or actress you're creating content about, which is why it's important to think about whether that person works for your audience. I read a piece about some behind-the-scenes discussions at *Wired* magazine which talks about how they're going to write a piece about *Being John Malkovich* screenwriter Charlie Kaufman. In it, they talk about Kaufman being a *Wired* guy – someone their readership has an interest in and affinity with. Charlie Kaufman, brilliant though he is, doesn't really matter to a Yahoo Movies audience. But Tom Hiddleston does.

The boffin

I love writing these pieces, and the guys at Yahoo gave them to me frequently as a result. I think using someone who is an expert in something of actual value to talk about matters as ephemeral as movies lends whatever you're writing credibility and depth, and it also means that your audience will be able to take away something interesting from the piece to talk about in the pub with their friends. Takeaway is important – it's what solidifies the success of a feature in your reader's mind, which is more likely to pull them back to your page/magazine/writing/Facebook timeline in the future. Plus, I always learned something new, which was enjoyable. Using this technique, I've written about everything from who would really win between a Predator and an Alien, to how Hollywood gets science wrong, via will Skynet take over the world like in *The Terminator* and why *Goldfinger* is the perfect Bond movie. Finding an expert tends to be fairly easy – I generally go straight to Waterstones and see which author has written on the subject I'm researching. Otherwise, you'll often find University College London (UCL) professors in my work. That's because the university has a brilliant 'find an expert' database with contact details and areas of expertise. Plus they tend to have a sense of humour, which is useful when you're asking them whether it's really possible to survive a nuclear explosion by hiding in a lead-lined fridge.

Lateral thinking

Kong: Skull Island is set in the 1970s, so you could do something about seventies movie tropes. Or the original 1933 *King Kong* featured breakthrough stop-motion animation work by iconic genius Ray Harryhausen, so you could do something about the best stop-motion effects in cinema. While this is only tenuously connected to the film you're ostensibly writing about, you'll still get traffic because of your headline or sell (the bit beneath your headline which sums up what your article is about).

In fact, this broader approach to the film is how we came up with the feature I ended up writing. *Kong: Skull Island* is part of a series with the giant ape as the protagonist. The deputy editor, Tom, initially came up with the idea of writing about all the King Kong movies there'd ever been (there's been *Son of Kong* in 1933 and a 1962 Japanese matchup against Godzilla). But once I'd looked through his list and seen that there was a rubbishy 1986 sequel called *King Kong Lives* featuring monkey romance and starring Linda Hamilton from *The Terminator*, it was clear that our take should be "The terrible Kong movie you've never seen". Ideally it would have included an interview with someone from the film, but I couldn't get anyone to return my calls apart from co-writer Steven Pressfield, who pointed me towards some humorous self-deprecation he'd written in a memoir about the experience rather than a full-blown chat. Still, it made for a funny story with some excellent gifs. I wasn't overly mean about it, but suitably incredulous at the dubious storytelling.

Anniversaries and birthdays

Anniversaries are a bonanza for entertainment feature story ideas. There are reasons why they're used for anything from daily radio segments to long-form magazine articles: (a) they're happening constantly; (b) they tap into nostalgia which audiences generally like; (c) there's usually pictures to accompany such ideas, so one can actually execute them in a visually interesting way; (d) the talent associated with them is normally easier to get a hold of if you want to get a new perspective. The list goes on …

I use them frequently, particularly when I'm trying to come up with film ideas. To illustrate, I flicked through a couple of notebooks and found a couple of pages of anniversary pitches I had taken into Yahoo commissioning meetings. I thought it would be useful to recreate them here. (Please be aware that these are initial brainstorms and in no way am I trying to tell you that these are brilliant or unique stories; it's just how I began the process.)

March 8 1996 Fargo – *doco woman who died/treasure urban myth*

The way I dug up these movie anniversaries was simple – Wikipedia has a pretty good list of the films that were released at different points during a particular year. I would scour that list going back 10, 20, 25 or 30 years, normally, to see if anything popped. February/March tended to be a less good time as that's notoriously when studios dump the films they think are going to be flops. But that clearly wasn't the case with the Coen brothers' classic *Fargo*, which is one of the great modern noirs. With this idea, it was less about the Coens themselves, who don't necessarily scream Yahoo, and more to do with a documentary I'd inadvertently happened across while researching something else. In it was a woman who supposedly travelled to – and died – at the movie's location because she appeared to mistakenly believe that the film's treasure was actually real and still buried somewhere under the snowy landscapes of North Dakota. That kind of quirky story, while not totally original, felt like something that could appeal to a Yahoo audience who weren't au fait with the Channel 4 doco schedules.

March 15 1996 Ed – *Matt Le Blanc/chimp*

Joey from *Friends*. A monkey. Had possibilities.

February 19 1986 Parting Glances – *seminal LGBT film*

Again, this didn't feel particularly Yahoo, but the editor was open to the occasional think piece and was interested in educating his audience from time to time as well.

February 28 1986 Pretty in Pink – *Brat Pack hangers-on*

This shouted "Where are they now?" photo gallery to me.

March 31 2006 Basic Instinct 2 – *David Morrissey quote*

Proving how it's always worth remembering the best interviews and filing away funny stories or quotes you've been given, seeing the title *Basic Instinct 2* made me immediately think of a chat I had with the actor David Morrissey in 2007 for a mediocre thriller called *The Reaping*. Towards the end of the interview, we got onto his favourite ever day as an actor and – I'm paraphrasing here – his answer was the day he spent shooting a love scene with Sharon Stone for the much-derided *Basic Instinct* sequel before watching his football team Liverpool come back from a three-goal deficit in the 2005 Champions League final to win the cup on penalties. I thought if I could find that quote somewhere in my notes, it might act as the catalyst for some kind of feature.

March 13 1992 My Cousin Vinny – *Tomei accidental Oscar myth*

There's long been an urban myth that the only reason Marisa Tomei won the Best Supporting Actress Academy Award for this comedy is because the presenter Jack Palance read out the wrong name on the card (something we know to be false if the 2017 *Moonlight* Oscar mix-up furore is anything to go by). It seemed like it could be the launching pad for a story about award myths, or similar.

March 20 1992 Basic Instinct – *what happened to the erotic thriller?*

Another think piece, this time about a genre that seemed to be huge in the 1980s and 1990s, basically before the Internet and broadband meant that audiences could get access to sex any time they wanted on their laptops.

Stallone – *Over The Top* salary/weird sports

I think I'd been banging on about this dreadful film for a while. For anyone that doesn't know it (almost everyone), it's a 1987 drama about a trucker who makes money arm-wrestling while trying to rebuild his relationship with his estranged son. It's only notable because it's (a) a sports movie about arm-wrestling and (b) Stallone got paid £9.5 million for it – a deal which is thought to have altered star salaries forever and precipitated the rise of the $20 million-per-movie performer. As such, I thought we could have gone multiple ways with this story – depending on the tack.

None of these ended up getting written, but they meant as a writer, I was able to take plentiful ideas into the pitch meeting, which is important.

The diary

Being up to date with the entertainment diary is fundamental to your success in this line of work. While diary events in and of themselves aren't breaking news, you should be using them to get it. Back when I started in the industry, you really relied on these premium services to sort out your week and month. London At Large or its then rival Celeb Bully as we called it (now known as FENS Celebrity) gave you and your forward-planning team a simple way to figure what was coming out when and who was going to be around to talk about it. These things still exist and have even expanded their goals to include more content. There's the Press Association diary and sites like Celebrity Intelligence. But they've been somewhat usurped by social media and the fact that material is shared differently now. Nevertheless, while I wouldn't necessarily advocate splashing out largish sums on this kind of thing, I would suggest that one of the things you need to become very good at very quickly is knowing what's going on. Forward planning is the thing that everyone needs to be doing all the time but no one seems to have the time for. Knowing what's coming will allow you time to approach the requisite PR and ask for accreditation, giving you options if you don't get into certain things but still need content. It will also mean that if you're freelance, you're able to start pitching ideas early, getting in before other people. And it's also vital for uncovering gems. That might be a Middle Eastern film festival so you can think of stories for Arab-based English-language newspaper *The National*, or it could mean being allowed to film at a fan convention so you can make some funny viral cosplay videos for an online outlet.

Understanding your diary will also telegraph your year. The Oscars are going to be on this date, which means that editors will be starting to brainstorm a month or two beforehand. Cannes is between then and then, which means you need to get your press application in by such-and-such a day. Coachella is here and Primavera is there. Carefully filed emails from publicists will help with all this once you get on the right lists (don't delete everything you receive out of hand), but make sure you're also combing through Launchingfilms.com and baseorg.uk, which list the theatrical movie release schedule and, in the case of the latter, focus on the home entertainment sector. While this won't necessarily give you in-depth information on junkets and premieres, it'll at least alert you and let you do some more digging and research. Following TV channel PR departments on Twitter will also be a big help. It can be a tedious job and one that often feels like drawing up an elaborate revision timetable with multiple pens and colours when you should just be memorising the periodic table and reading *The Taming of the Shrew*. But if you do it right and you utilise the data you accrue as a result, it'll be worth it.

Conclusion

Last year, my second-year students at Coventry University made a meme of me – my face transplanted onto every character from a group shot of the CBeebies show *Balamory* with the caption "What's the story, Balamory?"

I think I was right to be pleased by it. I'd spent the previous six months haranguing them at every opportunity to think about whether what they were pitching for their assignments was a good story – if it was something that stood out or felt like it had a new angle. Mostly at the beginning, it wasn't. But when they realised that I wasn't going to shut up about it, even when they looked annoyed or bored, they got better. They pushed themselves harder. There were raised voices, even tears, stories of late-night anxiety when another potential interviewee who would have been really interesting failed to return an email or said no officially.

The key to those who were ultimately successful was simple. They didn't stop. They continued banging down the door, or they thought of a different way into the house. They went away and came back with a fresh batch of ideas. To them I'd say it was worth it. And if you do the same, I'd say as much to you.

Ten top tips – getting the scoop and breaking stories

1. Fake it till you make it. You're not the only person who's been terrified about picking up a phone or asking a difficult question. But the difference between a successful journalist and one who isn't is not necessarily their writing ability or their contact list – it's the ability to find people and talk to them. If you're good at that, you'll do well. If that scares you, fine. Pretend it doesn't until it really doesn't.

2. Don't rely on the diary. It can be a useful tool for entertainment journalism, but speaking to people about possible stories can be just as effective.

3. Avoid the churn. So much of entertainment journalism can be aggregation – reworking something from a press release or from another website, acting as a point of breaking release news or the like. That's fine up to a point. But what will really make you stand out is approaching a story from a unique angle or adding something to it which nobody has previously thought of. That might be getting a few quotes from someone (not necessarily a celebrity, but, for example, a boffin who can put your news in context) or positioning the story in a clever way.

4. Think about the headline – and by the headline I mean the angle of the story. How will your audience interact with what you've created? Is there an interesting way in for them or will it stand out on their Facebook feed?

5. If you think it's a good story, don't be put off. Be tenacious and do your best to get it. Believe me, the feeling of 'getting' a great story is one of the biggest highs you'll have as a journalist.

6. There'll be a lot of false starts. Young journalists often seem to think that whatever story idea they have, it'll work and they'll find excellent people to comment for it. I can guarantee that won't be the case. Be prepared to be working on multiple story ideas. Sometimes you'll put many hours into them and you'll still have to abandon them because it turns out you can't get a hold of a good interviewee, the story's moved on or you realise you were wrong in the first place and it's actually a boring idea! If that's the case, don't fret. It's frustrating, but it's part of the job. And it's not wasted time. You will have learned something as a result.

7. Buy yourself a planner. It's important to keep a good track of everything you have going on.

8. Maintaining sources, contacts and your social media feed is a full-time job. Be prepared to put in the work.

9. It's often said that observation is one of a journalist's most valuable assets. It's probably the *most* important. Even when you're working on something

specific, keep your eyes and ears – or nose! – peeled for what else is going on around you. Sometimes the best stories are the ones which creep up on you.

10. Remember your audience. Will this work for them? What do they need from it and how will you provide that for them? A good question to ask yourself: why are *you* writing this story *now*?

MELANIE BROMLEY – CHIEF CORRESPONDENT, *E! NEWS*

What would you say to a person looking to break into the profession right now?

> To learn as much about the profession as possible. Maximise the amount of skills you have. Don't limit yourself. Don't think that you just want to be an on-air correspondent or just an editor or just a writer. Those single-skill jobs just won't exist in the future.
>
> It's important that you are able to do everything, no matter whether you chose to be a print journalist, a broadcast journalist or an online journalist. You need to be able to do all of it. Start to follow journalists and brands you admire on social media; look at how they are using various platforms in different ways to deliver the news. Monitor what they are doing on Facebook versus Snapchat, how they tell their story on Twitter – notice the differences in the way they package stories.

What are the three most important things you need as a broadcast news journalist?

1. Network. The most important thing in journalism is to know as many people as possible. Attend events where you are going to cross paths with people who may be able to help you, whether in your career or with a story. And be in contact with your sources even when you don't need them for a story.
2. Be curious. Literally read anything and everything about the beat you want to cover, especially from publications that you wouldn't normally go to. Notice point of view; that's becoming very important in news. If you are covering a story, what is going to be your unique angle? How will you be additive to the story? How will you bring something different to the topic?
3. Be cynical, but in a good way. I am a very positive person, but I never take things at face value. I always ask the who, what, where, when in order to really understand what lies beneath. It's this skill that helps you move on a story, understand the motivation of sources and comprehend why a certain story matters.

What do you know now that you wish you'd known when you became an entertainment journalist?

How technology has changed the business. My biggest regret is not embracing new media at the beginning, which meant I had some catching up to do. I am still not on Snapchat, and at this point it just feels too complicated for me to get to grips with, but obviously I can't avoid it forever. I will get to it soon.

How do you see the future of your profession and what might a young person need to know moving forward?

Be flexible. Journalism is changing rapidly. Not just the way we deliver and package news, but also the way we tell a story. Subscribe to journalism/tech websites, keep an eye on the changes and adapt your skills to meet future needs.

What's the best thing about your job?

I work both on camera and behind the camera (which is still slightly unusual in entertainment news). I love being able to tell the stories myself that I report and not rely on other people's insight. I never use a prompter and am often live. It means I have to always know exactly what I am talking about; I can't fake it.

Tell us about your favourite moments in your job?

Covering the royal wedding, the births of George and Charlotte – it's just wonderful to be there as history is being made.

And it's rather gruesome but I always love when we have a very big story (last year, Prince's death). Something of significance to general news outlets as well as entertainment ones because then it means I am on deadline and trying to beat not just our usual competitors but everyone, and that's a huge adrenalin buzz, especially if you manage to scoop them all.

(Interview with author, 2017)

2

ENTERTAINMENT JOURNALISM – IN CONTEXT

One Sunday evening in June 1950, top US TV star Lucille Ball and her husband Desi Arnaz sat down to listen to Walter Winchell's compulsive weekly radio gossip column. Like most Americans, the Arnaz duo enjoyed Winchell's machine-gun delivery and snappy language as he dished the dirt on the public and private lives of Hollywood's stars. But their cosy evening in was shattered when Winchell announced in his usual barking style that Ball was expecting a "blessed event". Though the hack could talk at a dizzying rate of 197 words per minute (the way he wrote was nicknamed 'slanguage' for its unusual informality), Lucy and Desi knew they hadn't misheard – after several miscarriages and a hopeful pregnancy test that had recently gone off to the lab, this was how they were to find out they were expecting a baby. Wily Winchell's far-reaching contacts included a medical mole on the lookout for splash-worthy test results. Though she later made light of the exposé to silence the baying press ("If Winchell says so, it's gotta be true!" she joked), Ball never forgave Winchell for stealing an utterly private moment from her to offer up for public consumption. When he later accused her of being a Communist during the McCarthy witch-hunts and she was asked how the gossip hound was able to uncover such secrets, she replied bitterly, "Walter Winchell knew I was pregnant before I did."

Winchell's scoop is still a revelation even by today's Internet-buzzing standards, where pop stars and actresses are routinely outed as pregnant or addicts within hours of discovering the news themselves. But it is fitting his greatest scoop should concern a Hollywood pregnancy (still hotcake-selling news as many celebs can attest) seeing as Winchell pioneered the very notion of modern celebrity gossip, where the sexual activity of an action hero is as important as their close-up and where the loose words of a starlet stumbling out of a nightclub are as headline-grabbing as her film debut.

Lucy and Desi's indignant dismay that personal news was shared with their fascinated public is one example of what is now a routine aspect of the fame game thanks to Winchell's stance on making the private lives of celebrities fair game for audience amusement. No actor or pop queen worth their salt can now expect to be left alone – their dates, engagements, marriages, divorces, affairs, births, deaths, weight fluxes and bad hair days are fodder for our insatiable appetite to know everything about our heroes. They are even told things they *didn't* know, as ex-Spice Girl Mel B discovered in 2006 when she learnt that Eddie Murphy, her current boyfriend and father of her unborn baby, was seeing another woman. In true Winchell style, Mel wasn't told that her relationship was over by Murphy or a friend. The news broke to the public on the Web as she flew across the Atlantic to be greeted at LAX with the news that Murphy had turned out on the red carpet with another girlfriend on his arm. Walter would have been proud.

Winchell was not the first to expose the infidelities, romances, pregnancies and deviancies of the rich and famous – he simply refined and glamorised it, linking it inextricably to Hollywood and a burgeoning movie business. As early as 1729, founding father Benjamin Franklin, creator of America's free press, began feeding the public's appetite for gossip with his scandal-laden and sensational slap in the face to the era's puritanical sobriety, *The Pennsylvania Gazette*. Though a paper primarily for business tips and news about a constantly changing new continent, Franklin also gave space to stories of infidelity and lurid crime, claiming that printers "sometimes print vicious or silly things not worth reading, [but] it may not be because they approve of such things themselves, but because the people are so viciously and corruptly educated" (Franklin, 1731). Like many a gossip editor and publisher to come after him, Franklin excused his publishing of scandal as merely providing a salacious and eager public with the stories they wanted to read. This carried on in the following decades and grew even more popular in the years following the Civil War as the private lives of It girl Lillie Langtry or boxer John L. Sullivan became tabloid fodder. As Christopher B. Daly writes,

> For the readers, especially those urban readers who found themselves living among crowds of strangers, news about such celebrities offered a common topic of conversation, a way of appearing to be in the know. Up until then, people had gossiped about their actual neighbours; now, when they came together in taverns, or on the factory floor, or in the trolley car, they could participate confidently in discussions about the personal foibles and heroic qualities of people they had never met but only read about in the papers.
>
> *(Daly, 2012)*

It was happening in Britain too. *The Pall Mall Gazette* used to run celebrity profiles by the bucketload in the 1880s, while in a precursor to Andy Warhol's *Interview* magazine in which famous people spoke to other famous people, the *Gazette* had Mark Twain interviewed by Rudyard Kipling in 1889. In 1904, the *Illustrated Daily Mirror* (the progenitor of UK tabloid the *Mirror*) changed from a so-called woman's paper – with a predominantly female staff running a lot of lifestyle content – to what was known as a 'picture paper'. The first issue, published on 2 April, featured shots of the then Royal family. Not much has changed since.

By the time Winchell started his craft, every newspaper routinely ran tales of dishonour and humiliation alongside the politics and horse racing. But in the 1920s, society tittle-tattle gave way to a new breed of dirt-dishing that would change 20th-century journalism – and audience expectation – forever. Winchell's success also allowed media owners to see how much money was in this kind of journalism – by June 1929, Winchell was working for Hearst tabloid the *Mirror*, earning a staggering $500 per week (that's £5500 today) plus 50% of any syndication profits from his column. It wasn't just about voyeurism though. At the beginning of the 20th century, so-called 'yellow journalism' – described by P. David Marshall as "stories that were both sensational and closer to the every day lives of [the] new urban readership" (Marshall, 2005) – was at the centre of much of the media empires of William Randolph Hearst and Joseph Pulitzer. But as Marshall continues, "Celebrities represented heightened examples of individual achievement and transformation and thereby challenged the rigidity of class-based societies by presenting the potential to transcend these categories." What's more, he says, "Consumer culture, through advertisements, department stores and the actual expanded range of products and services, presented a diverse array of possibilities for modern individuals to make themselves anew." In other words, this was something very similar to the 'anybody can be a celebrity' culture we have today thanks to the rise of social media and reality television. There were particular hives of tabloid activity too. In the early 1930s, future journalistic icon Hugh Cudlipp was a reporter for a Manchester paper in the British seaside resort Blackpool, where the Pleasure Beach became a source of showbiz fodder. It may not be an entertainment haunt anymore – or least not one which appeals to mainstream media outlets – but back when Ripley's Believe It Or Not opened there in 1931, it was a source of many stories.

Winchell sat alongside other gossip columnists such as Los Angeles-based gossip mavens Louella Parsons and Hedda Hopper, and paved the way for ear-to-the-ground institutions Army Archerd and Ed Sullivan, plus a slew of tabloid publications such as *Confidential*; but Winchell remained the king of scandal with a withering turn of phrase and a fearsome ability to uncover shameful, private and illegal skeletons. "I usually get my stuff from people who promised somebody else that they would keep it a secret," he boasted. Of course, Walter was an expert in secrets – his own life was hardly a fairy tale, and his vindictive attacks on his perceived enemies such as 'pinko' Lucille Ball or New York radio host Barry Gray (who he disparagingly referred to as "Borey Pink") were symptomatic of a man struggling with his own personal scandals and familial megalomania.

Married to fellow board-treader Rita Greene in 1919, Winchell had drifted apart from his wife and sired an illegitimate daughter with his lover, June Magee, before his divorce was final. Throughout the hush-hush divorce proceedings, Walter and June had pretended to be married, and they continued the high-pressure charade for the rest of their lives because Winchell was afraid that marrying officially would expose the fact his daughter, named for him as Walda, was a bastard. It was not the only thing Winchell jealously kept private. As Walda grew into adolescence, she suffered psychologically and frequented various discreet mental institutions (not something one would want polite society to know). Walter guarded Walda vociferously throughout her life, possibly in part to preserve his own stature, and he even went so far as to break up her imminent marriage because he didn't deem it a suitable match. Mental instability and illegitimacy were not the only scandal to dog Winchell's family. His son, Walter Jr, suffered the ignominy of rising to the career high of restaurant dishwasher before committing suicide on Christmas Eve, 1968. Hardly the bright future Walter hoped for his namesake, who claimed that he was a freelance writer rather than a man who rinsed plates. It was the final nail in the Winchell's showbiz coffin. Already broken by ridicule after his gung-ho support of (and, in some cases, collusion with) Senator McCarthy's Communist witch-hunts as well as the failure of his weekly TV show, the scandal and tragedy of Walter Jr's death prompted Winchell to retire in 1969.

Of course, some celebrity hacks took Winchell's desire for personal anonymity one step further by hiding behind a pseudonym. William Conner wrote under the name "Cassandra" for decades in the *Daily Mirror*, with Cassandra even losing a libel case in 1956 with the popular entertainer Liberace after the paper outed him as homosexual in a brutal and offensive article. Even though the performer was gay, he didn't admit it to anyone publicly and was worried that doing so would affect his success. The trial ended in the jury finding for Liberace and awarding him £8000 in damages (equivalent to £500,000 today).

Though he was posthumously inducted into the Radio Hall of Fame and his obituaries in 1972 hailed a trailblazer of modern gutter journalism, by the time Winchell bowed out of the tittle-tattle rat run, he was no longer king of the scoop. He had spawned an entire industry and redefined the culture of celebrity. The world was full of his progeny – gossipmongers taking scandal, revelations and personal vendettas to new highs and lows. The first issue of *People*, published on 25 February 1974, had Mia Farrow on the cover. Its launch editor Richard Stolley describes its ethos: "Young is better than old. Pretty is better than ugly. Rich is better than poor. TV is better than music. Music is better than movies. Movies are better than sports. And anything is better than politics." (*Chicago Tribune*, 1991) *Rolling Stone* owner Jann Wenner bought *Us Weekly* in 1985, telling writer Edwin Diamond of *New York Magazine* that the reason was: "Call it what you want – gossip journalism, celebrity journalism, human interest journalism. By any name, this has become the dominant theme of American journalism over the last five years." (Diamond, 1985) In the UK, Rupert Murdoch bought and relaunched *The Sun* in 1969, adding the showbiz column known as Bizarre in 1982 (it's interesting to note too that several tabloid editors have emerged from Bizarre, including Piers Morgan and Dominic Mohan). The *Daily Mail* ostensibly became a tabloid in 1971, and with the rise of the *News of the World*, news as entertainment – or entertainment as news – was firmly on the agenda of the mainstream British press.

Walter may have opened Pandora's box, looking to Hollywood as the Babylon of smut and secrets, but his successors would uncover, manipulate and bury the juiciest stories of the day and feed a public appetite for famous dirty laundry.

While cross-pollination between gossipmonger and star has always been a factor of tittle-tattle (Hedda and Louella always traded salacious titbits with their quarry and willingly boosted stars as favours), the lines of battle have stayed relatively drawn. It's 'them and us' – the celebrity trying to shape their coverage, via a team of fixers, lawyers and ego masseurs, versus the press (and public) trying to uncover what they don't want us to know.

But in the 21st century, those lines are ebbing, flowing and blurring to the point of confusion. Though all parties may continue to deny it, secretive but mutually beneficial alliances between the predator and their prey are more prevalent than ever. In reality, the paparazzi and gossip rags so loathed in celebrity sound bites are a vital tool in image-shaping and press control. New loves are announced, family images re-enforced, weight loss celebrated and splits announced by way of 'stolen' shots.

Most importantly, it often gives the famous, whose personalities are inherently controlling, the ability to disseminate information in the way *they* want it delivered. Nicole Kidman would have seemed bitter and callous had she released a statement at the end of her marriage to Tom Cruise in 2001 saying that she was glad to be rid of him. Instead, she tipped off a photographer about when she would be leaving her lawyer's office after the divorce became final. As such, the world saw Miss Kidman's girlish relief that the ordeal was over with an open-armed pose of liberation, but without her having to be directly negative. Her career subsequently soared as a victim of the break-up, while Cruise's cachet declined. "Celebrities know you are only as valuable as your last big thing," says Hollywood therapist Stacy Kaiser, "If there hasn't been a big thing, they will work to create attention and press in other ways to maintain or increase their celebrity."

Whilst personal publicists complain about the media's interest in their clients' private lives, most photo agencies admit that they wouldn't turn a profit if not for the complicity of the stars' managers and PR teams. That Hollywood studio system has never gone away – publicists will trade the whereabouts of an A-list client in return for covering of one of their lesser-known stars. According to Jane Ennis of *Now* magazine, "Some of [these stars] haven't done anything of any talent or ability for years. They're kept alive by behaving outrageously, getting photographed and those shots appearing in the papers." (In Young, 2006)

And it's not just the fame-hungry and brazen who are playing ball in this exchange of information. Even someone like supposedly press-loathing actress Gwyneth Paltrow dances with the tabloid press to manage their news. After Oscar-winner Paltrow gave birth to daughter Apple in 2004, she and husband Chris Martin knew that there would be a bounty on a picture of their baby – so tipped off British paparazzo Steve Sands. Sands took 'surprise' shots of the pair coming out of the London hospital where she had delivered and sold the pictures to *People* magazine for $125,000, Managing Editor Larry Hackett having been aware of the fakery. Janice Min, former editor-in-chief of *Us Weekly*, has been frank about the deception: "I would probably say at least 50 per cent of what you see in terms of Hollywood coverage is something that was not necessarily born organically. This is how celebrities survive." (In Hagan and Marr, 2006)

The insatiable appetite for snatched shots of our stars has engendered a further craving for the new style pap shot – one that would never have been seen in Walter Winchell's day. Then, audiences ate up pictures of their matinee idols to see just how good they looked and to aspire to be like them, and they believed that these people were blessed with a certain star quality your average Joe in the street could never obtain. Now in a world of round-the-clock gossip and pap shots, the aim is reversed. Now audiences want to shatter the illusion of their favourite stars, demystify them and scorn them for being too fat, too thin, having a 'wardrobe malfunction', sweating profusely, wearing the wrong thing. Audiences want to see celebrities make mistakes, to democratise the star status so the stunning actress who may earn $6 million a picture and be married to the *People*'s Sexiest Man Alive is essentially no better than any 'civilian', because she is fallible. Just like anyone else, this girl gets lipstick on her teeth, sports patchy fake tan or falls off her platform heels rolling out of a nightclub. This new way of things was pared down to a single moment by Mark Frith in his diaries charting his time as editor of *heat* magazine. He points to Wednesday 26 February 2003, when rival *Now* magazine featured three women on their cover (including *Friends* star Lisa Kudrow and Nicole Kidman) looking, well, less than their usual red carpet best. The headline was: "ROUGH! Even stars have bad days". Frith initially thought the gambit was a huge error as it wasn't glamorous. But the issue went on to sell 730,000 copies, a gigantic hit. "That cover changed everything in the celebrity magazine market," he writes. "It shows that readers want their celebs to look awful rather than good." (Frith, 2008)

And in times of war, terror and recession, audiences rely more on entertainment and celebrity to take them momentarily away from real life. "It's always easier to distract from your own life by focusing on someone else's," says Kaiser. "Gossip also allows us to bond with our friends and family."

The concept of celebrity schadenfreude may be a modern conceit – and a world away from the golden age of Hollywood idolisation – but it is, says Kaiser, simply a natural progression for an inquisitive and communicative human race. "People have gossiped since the beginning of time," she says. "Before we had access to celebrity dirt, we just talked about neighbours and friends." Now we can simply do it bigger, faster, brighter …

With both the rise of interest in celebrity news and the ubiquity of the Internet, one of the most significant yet inevitable changes in the way gossip is reported is the advent of the entertainment blog website. The success of these sites – like PerezHilton.com, created by Mario Lavendeira, Just Jared and previously places like thesmokinggun.com, founded by former *Village Voice* reporters William Bastone and Daniel Green – means that as well as spawning endless imitators, they are no longer merely reporting the showbiz news agenda – they're driving it. It's a situation not everyone's happy about.

NATASHA BIRD – DIGITAL EDITOR, *ELLE*

What would you say to a person looking to break into your profession right now?

As with all areas of journalism, it's a pretty tough industry to break into. I routinely get 300 to 400 applicants for every new open role on my team that I advertise. Plus, even in the highest ranks of journalism, it's not a super well-paid career. I don't mean to be terribly off-putting – rather, get into it only if you absolutely love it.

Be prepared to try your hand at lots of different areas of journalism (I've personally been a reporter, a foreign correspondent, in print and now a digital expert). Come to every situation with a 'can-do' attitude and leave your ego and entitlement at the door.

What are the three most important things you need as a digital editor?

1. You need to be prepared to work antisocial hours – the Internet doesn't sleep, so if there's an important awards ceremony happening in California at 1 a.m. GMT, you need to be prepared to drink a lot of coffee and suck it up, because if you're not first to the best story of the night, someone else will be and then you've lost.
2. As a digital editor, I am also a team manager. One of the most important things I am careful to do when building my team is look for keen, savvy, eagle-eyed, talented writers who aren't just good at crafting stories, but who are also clued up on all things tech and digital. So many managers are scared to hire people that are better than them at things, but in digital – a world that moves at crazy-fast pace – the more you can arm your team with great, ambitious, talented recruits, the better the position you will be in as a brand. Every one of my team is better than me at some skill or other; that's why I hired them.
3. Resilience. The Internet is a cruel place and a clever place. Someone will always be ready to troll you, and some other person will always be there to pip you to the post. So you need to have tough skin and a positive attitude to not get brought down and to fight back and do something even better with your site the next day.

What do you know now that you wish you'd known when you became a digital editor?

I don't have any regrets, and I am pretty pleased with the learning process that has been my whole career. However, I would advise anyone getting into the digital sphere to try your hand at working in a big corporation that is getting it right before you set up shop on your own (as I tried to do a number of years ago).

Access to SEO (search engine optimisation) experts, social media gurus, developers, ad operations teams and also the budget that a big publishing house can give you are invaluable and will really change how you view the digital market. Trying to do all of that on your own with not a lot of time or money is like running before you can walk.

How do you see the future of your profession and what might a young person need to know moving forward?

Digital journalism changes all the time – literally every day. One of the best things you can be is adaptive. Only those who adapt quickly will survive. So if you're one of the people who likes routine and is regularly heard saying "But, this is the way we were taught to do it before", then get out!

What's the best thing about your job?

Oh, there are so many things to love about working on the Internet. They are probably the same things that would scare other people – like immediate feedback, the constantly changing climate, being able to watch the numbers change from minute to minute. It makes losses really hard to take, especially when grappling with a new Facebook algorithm that seems to be biased against what you do, but it also makes the wins really tangible and calculable.

I think the team's solidarity is actually greater on a digital publication – typically smaller teams, who have to work some silly hours at a fast pace – it rather bonds you together. We're a tight-knit unit. But then again, I can't speak for all teams.

Tell us about your favourite moments in your job?

It's journalism, so you get amazing access to people. Altruistically, I am proud of some of our big campaigns. The ones where you feel like you might actually help change the tide of opinion in society – like our *ELLE* #MoreWomen feminism campaign to get more women a seat at the table in parliament and in board rooms.

But also I've done some great interviews. Having an argument with Tom Hardy, playing 'name the body part' with Channing Tatum, challenging Mark Wahlberg to be a better feminist, that sort of thing.

(Interview with the author, 2017)

"Perez Hilton is a mean man," wrote singer Lily Allen on Twitter in 2008 after Hilton suggested (without clarification) there was something suspicious about Allen's miscarriage. "I don't know what I did to piss him off. [...] It's not fair to say I'm washed up and it's not fair to make up these feuds between people. [Perez] writes things that aren't true with no shame about it and that's sad." (In Stosuy, 2008)

We've noted the gap between star and public has grown ever more narrow, and proponents of 'citizen journalism' like Hilton have done the same for the reporter and consumer. There have always been snitchers, tippers, sources and 'onlookers' to facilitate the discovery of secrets of the rich and famous; but the new wave of celebrity bloggers have taken the idea of the confidential journalistic source and pushed it one step further, actively encouraging interactivity with its readers. Every reader can now shape the story by reporting on what they heard a star whisper in a quiet restaurant, who was spotted buy what at the store and even who is a generous tipper and who stiffs the waiting staff.

"It's all changed so much," Melanie Bromley, a former *Us Weekly* west coast editor, now chief correspondent at *E! Entertainment*, tells me.

> It's actually forced us to re-evaluate how we do things, even though at an American magazine the vetting process has long-held and heavily enforced strictures, like named sources and things like that. But while the competition is tough – and it's been infuriating when Perez scoops us with something we've had for a while but can't totally stand up – it's reinvigorated the media process. Although I'm sure it's made it tougher for the celebs.

The lengths these sites are prepared to push stories have indeed forced the magazines to follow suit. Sites criticising fashion choices, pointing out sweat stains or showcasing make-up-free faces have influenced news stand titles to adapt similarly. Now a starlet cannot accidentally wear the same dress as another red carpet walker without the two being held up in a competition as to "who wore it best".

And woe betide any star having a wardrobe, make-up or personal hygiene crisis while out and about. The Web's power to zoom and highlight photos mean every inch is now under scrutiny, resulting in schoolyard put-downs and, in some cases, distasteful cruelty. Britney Spears, then media punchbag, experienced this in early 2008 when she faced rumours she was expecting another child. Bloggers soon found a way of proving she was not by zooming in on a shot of Spears getting out of a car while inadvertently flashing her underwear. No surprise, but eagle-eyed star-watchers noted that extreme close-up revealed a blood-stained sanitary towel. "At least we know she's not pregnant!" the headlines ran.

The more flexible and cavalier laws of the Web, which have yet to be fully detailed and codified, have changed the way we approach gossip. Where a magazine or paper has to ensure its stories are legally sound, websites can report a story in progress, updating and/or apologising as they go. "What would be the point of holding back?" Nick Denton, who founded Gawker Media in 2002, told *The*

Guardian in 2006, years before the company was brought down as a result of the Hulk Hogan sex tape lawsuit.

> We're independent, we're not owned by a big media company, we don't have to abide by the standards that have been set down a generation ago, we have enough advertising to pay the bills and we attract a very desirable audience which seems to like the fact that we push things too far.
>
> *(Denton cited in Silver, 2006)*

Because surfers are exposed to so much and such invasive gossip on the Net, our appetite and capacity for celeb titbits has also grown, psychologist Stacy Kaiser says.

> We have access to gossip 24 hours a day, seven days a week; we can get addicted to it in some ways. That addiction is easily fed by internet updates. Some people rush to their computers or mobile devices the minute they wake up to check out the latest dish on celebrities.

Certainly with our increasingly sedentary lifestyles it's never been easier or quicker to find out who's doing what right now … during a lunch break, while supposedly studying, during a lull in emails.

"We go after sacred cows," posits Denton.

> We run stories on the basis of one anonymous source in many cases and a bit of judgment. We put it out there. We make it clear the level of confidence we have in a story. We ask for help [from readers]. We ask for corroboration, we ask for denials. Every single story is a work in progress, it's not meant to be final, it's like a reporter's notebook.
>
> *(Denton cited in Silver, 2006)*

Of course it could be argued that lack of due diligence is what cost him his company.

"You tell me something and I can put it up within minutes and nobody will ever find out your name," Perez Hilton has said. "There's no fear because I take what I do very seriously and I never reveal my sources, ever." (In Zulkey, 2006) But how does he choose what's legit and what's not? "It depends where I've gotten it from and whom I've gotten it from," he explains. Early on, he claimed that because he was only writing a personal blog, rather than running a commercial enterprise, he could write his gossip without fear of being sued. The publicity does him no harm either. "I love being singled out," he says. "It's just driving more awareness, more traffic to me. I'm not worried or afraid of anything."

These sites generate huge amounts of traffic. And they are breaking stories. The success led big businesses like AOL Time Warner to create TMZ.com, a cash-rich celeb gossip site. "When I was at the FT [*Financial Times*], I always thought the most interesting stories were the ones journalists told each other over a drink after deadline," says Denton.

> The stories they can't publish because they are too sensitive or because they have been told off the record, or because they only have one source or they can't be stood up. The truth is those are the stories people are really interested in, so why shouldn't those conversations be reflected in a publication?
>
> *(In Silver, 2006)*

This is guerrilla gossip – gone are the days of pussyfooting around publicists, exchanging secrets for juicier stories and staying friends with the star. "[There's] too much finagling with publicists, talent managers and other members of the industry's permanent government over who's going to grant an interview/appear on a cover," says William Bastone, a former *Village Voice* organised crime reporter who co-founded *thesmokinggun.com*. "Seems like nobody wants to step on anyone's feet." (In Romenesko, 2003)

Even the newspapers are starting to catch on that carefully crafted images are not what a far more media-savvy public want. British tabloids *The Sun* and the *Mirror* now update their pages throughout the day and don't solely rely on the content from that morning's edition. Mail Online, the Web version of the *Daily Mail*, relying primarily on showbiz and gossip, is one of the biggest English-language newspaper websites in the world. They know readers expect more. Mainstream sites too have got more prurient, far more alike in design and mentality to PerezHilton.com than before. The use of embedded video has been growing for some time and is now a crucial part of the system. Inevitably, this has led to TV spin-offs of the websites themselves. TMZ.com used to have a nightly syndicated gossip show. "It's become more monetised," says Perez, "there are more media outlets that are catering to interest that's always been there. People have wised up and realised they can profit from this inherent desire for celebrity." (In Zulkey, 2006) Gossip is now no longer a sweetener for the day's news, a column in a newspaper, a diversion for fifties housewives – it's big, BIG business, and willingly or not, we are all consumers.

As Errol Flynn once said, "It isn't what they say about you. It's what they whisper." I may have focused here on gossip or so-called celebrity journalism, but that's useful because it puts into context where the mindset of a showbiz-centric readership has been over the past century (and before). And the magazines, newspapers and TV shows I talk about here all featured 'proper' entertainment journalism, such as feature pieces, reviews and the like. Showbiz journalism has always got a bad rap, equated with gossip. And certainly there is crossover. The women's weeklies in the UK will do bona fide profiles, reviews and investigations, but they'll have a paparazzi picture on the front cover. *The Hollywood Reporter* will feature lengthy retrospectives and excellent creative roundtables (a group chat with a bunch of writers sitting around a, surprise, table), but will also talk about who's got married to whom and what someone's house is worth.

But while there may have always been gossip, there's also always been quality entertainment journalism. In US movie 'fan magazines' such as *Photoplay* and *Filmplay Journal* at the start of the 1920s, there was lots of quality writing, with iconic author H.L. Mencken acting as a film critic of *Screenland* in 1922. Author Anthony Slide even suggests that these kinds of magazines "often provided intellectual commentary to the statements of a star who had none" (Slide, 2010). The writings on popular culture by music critics like the *New Yorker*'s Alex Ross and Lester Bangs have become seminal non-fiction texts. British writer Charlie Brooker's reviews and columns have been collected and published as a stand-alone book.

Of course, there are too many outlets with quality entertainment and arts writing to mention here. When *Cosmopolitan* launched in Britain in 1972, it set the tone for well-crafted entertainment and lifestyle pieces (alongside more ephemeral material) in women's monthly glossy magazines. Heavyweight novelists like Norman Mailer wrote stories for *Playboy*. Pauline Kael became one of the most respected film critics of all time writing essays about Orson Welles or Martin Scorsese for the *New Yorker*. In the 1960s, Donald Zec wrote deeply personal profiles of stars like Marilyn Monroe for the *Mirror*, while into the 1980s and beyond, movie trade papers like *Screen International* covered the film industry like it was Parliament. Magazines such as *Empire, Rolling Stone, Melody Maker* and programmes like *The South Bank Show* have become highly successful and respected destinations for intelligent, funny, well-researched articles and segments about different forms of entertainment.

Yes, people love gossip about celebrities, but they also want a journalist to examine and evaluate the films these stars are in, explore a new genre of music taking off in a small English town, review the book everyone's reading on the train or explain just why this artist has become prizeworthy. And that's not likely to ever change.

The current landscape of entertainment journalism

There are some who still argue that entertainment journalism is some kind of 'lesser' discipline or that it doesn't matter as much as so-called hard news journalism. Looking objectively, of course covering a general election is more important than reviewing the latest Marvel movie or writing a celebrity profile of Justin Bieber. However, writes P. David Marshall,

> Journalism has been instrumental in proselytizing a new public sphere and celebrities have been a foundational means and method for the expansion of key elements of that new public sphere. In that convergence, journalism has expanded its "coverage" of entertainment and sports by developing features on personalities. It has also used techniques developed in writing about entertainment stars for its coverage of the famed and notorious in politics and many other domains.

> *(Marshall, 2005)*

In other words, entertainment journalism's emergence and evolution has directly affected the way all journalists work and how audiences interact with the material they produce. While you can debate the merits of that, you can't argue the impact. It matters.

Now though, it's a different beast to when Franchot Tone was a universal pin-up and Joan Crawford's divorce was announced in movie magazine *Modern Screen*; and it continues to mutate. As Martin Conboy writes in *The Press and Popular Culture*, "one of the most noticeable features of the current cultural scene is the erosion of the distinctions between popular and high culture and post-modernity's recognition of the ability of the popular to invade all spaces" (Conboy, 2001). This ties in with the current idea of 'content' over articles or TV packages and why a witty recap of a reality television show can sit alongside a serious piece about whitewashing in Hollywood movies and a review of the latest Ed Sheeran album on the same outlet.

Post Leveson, it's different even to when showbiz hacks like Sharon Marshall plied her trade in the late 1990s and early 2000s. In her memoir *Tabloid Girl*, Marshall remembers trying to get her first job on a red top newspaper. She took

> ten crates of Fosters to a national newspaper and stood next to them, waiting, CV in hand, until the news editor arrived at work. I blocked his route to the lifts, said I was the mad woman who rang every morning and that I would do anything, anything, to get a job on a tabloid newspaper. And I had brought beer.
>
> *(Marshall, 2010)*

Now the competition is probably even more fierce. In her autobiography, *Confessions of a Showbiz Reporter*, author Holly Forrest (a pseudonym) admits, "I realised a long time ago that if you want to get rich, my line of work isn't the way to do it. Being an entertainment reporter is all about marvelling at how rich other people are." (Forrest, 2013)

Forrest is also right about the rise of reader power thanks to the proliferation of high-speed Internet. There have always been 'cast lists' – the small selection of viable cover stars who are in essence driven by whether readers buy the issues with them on the front. It's why back in 2008 *Look* magazine might have rotated covers between Amy Winehouse, Jennifer Aniston, Angelina Jolie and Cheryl (then) Cole. It's why *Empire* magazine tends to fluctuate between Star Wars, Marvel and DC superheroes. But Forrest points to the top celebrity Google searches of 2012 being Kim Kardashian and Justin Bieber. She writes directly to her reader, saying,

> Kim Kardashian and Justin Bieber became global brands purely through the power of the internet; fans latched on to their appeal way before us in the press. … The media can still do a lot to fuel a showbiz fire, but more now than ever, what's hot is often out of our hands.
>
> *(Forrest, 2013)*

What were the 'winners' in 2016? Suffice to say, David Bowie, Pokémon GO and Prince were all in the top ten Google searches in that year.

This can be also be seen with the reduced impact of film reviews on, say, critically shruggable blockbusters like *Fast and Furious 8* or *Suicide Squad*, with the scale of the success of *Fifty Shades of Grey* or with the rise of YouTubers. What Forrest is saying, then, is that today's entertainment journalism is more interactive than it's ever been.

"With a largely free internet at our fingertips, the celebrity world is more accessible than ever," she writes.

> Who you spend your time looking up determines who we spend our time focusing on. If you resent that eminent scientists and liberal thinkers are missing from the list, start searching for a few and maybe we'll take notice. But that's the great thing about modern media: it's no longer so full of snobby journalists hiding out in their ivory towers, bleating about what they fancy and taking no notice of their audience. The internet's too transparent for that. These days, we're all in this showbiz world together.
>
> *(Forrest, 2013)*

NB: Since I can't cover everything about the history of entertainment journalism, I recommend some further reading:

Addison, A. (2017) *Mail Men: The Unauthorized Story of the* Daily Mail – *The Paper that Divided and Conquered Britain*. London: Atlantic Books.

Bernstein, S. (2006) *Mr Confidential: The Man, His Magazine and the Movieland Massacre that Changed Hollywood Forever*. London: Walford Press.

Best, K.N. (2017) *The History of Fashion Journalism*. London: Bloomsbury Academic.

Conboy, M. (2005) *Tabloid Britain*. New York: Routledge.

Conboy, M. (2011) *Journalism in Britain: A Historical Introduction*. London: Sage.

Epstein, E.J. (2014) *EXTRA: The Inventions of Journalism*. EJE Publications Ltd.

Thomson, D. (2016) *Television: A Biography*. New York: Thames and Hudson Ltd.

Wenner, J. (2017) *50 Years of Rolling Stone: The Music, Politics and People that Changed Our Culture*. New York: Abrams Books.

Ten top tips – entertainment and arts journalism in context

1. Don't labour under the misapprehension that entertainment journalism is a modern conceit. People have been doing this for years – and it's worth digging into the archives.

2. It may seem that the Web has changed journalism forever, but remember – the Internet is just a delivery system; journalism is the same as it ever was.

3. You must be a good reader to be a good writer. If you want to be a film reviewer, read Pauline Kael's books. If you're interested in being a showbiz

news reporter, check out Mark Frith's diaries. And don't shy away from long-form entertainment journalism either. *Easy Riders, Raging Bulls* by Peter Biskind, *High Concept* by Charles Fleming and *Final Cut* by Steven Bach are all highly recommended.

4. Learn from the mistakes of the past – outing people and attacking their politics in showbiz magazines should be consigned to history.

5. Think about why entertainment journalism is changing. Consider how the audience has fragmented and what that means as a content creator.

6. The complexity of media ownership is a subject oft overlooked by both the public and the journalists who work within the system. But be aware of it – it may inform unconscious bias or put you in ethically difficult situations. If you understand why that's happening, it will help you overcome it.

7. One of the important things about understanding the history of journalism is that it may make you better inclined to recognise where it might be going.

8. It's unlikely that any showbiz journalist will wield the same kind of power as someone like Louella Parsons or Walter Winchell ever again. So if you're getting into the industry to be someone like that, probably best to think again.

9. People love showbiz and celebrity, and that hasn't changed for decades. If you choose to do this as a job, while it may ebb and flow, the subject itself will always be there to write or create content about.

10. Tabloid journalism has always been sensationalist and over the top. Don't believe those who say it's worse now than it was.

ANDY WELCH – FREELANCE MUSIC JOURNALIST AND FEATURE WRITER

What would you say to a person looking to break into your profession right now?

Pick up as many skills as possible. When I graduated in 2004, people in a similar position to me now were telling me to learn HTML or how to use a video camera. While that was good advice, especially considering I've worked almost exclusively in online journalism since about 2007 – I don't think it went far enough.

Now, I would advise young journalists to immerse themselves in Photoshop, learn how to make gifs and become proficient with editing software such as Adobe Premiere.

Once upon a time journalists only wrote. Then came the Web and with it numerous CMS [content management systems]. But now, there's the rise in journalists having to double as 'content producers' (that dreaded word, 'content'), dabble with mobile apps and manage social media accounts – whether to make ends meet or because the job requires it. Having these skills in your arsenal is only going to make you more employable.

Media-related work is competitive at the best of times; today it's positively ruthless. Tool up!

What are the three most important things you need as a music journalist?

1. A unique voice. Okay, it's hard to be absolutely unique, but strive to find your own voice and don't fall into the traps of following critical consensus because you're scared to stand out or the equally atrocious trait of dismissing something out of hand just because you are hooked on appearing cool. If you think something's good, do it.
2. Brush up on history. Don't be in thrall to it – that's damaging and pointless – but knowing where contemporary music comes from is important. Challenge yourself with your listening, fill in gaps in your knowledge and aim to listen to almost as many perceived classics each week as new music.
3. Be bloody-minded. Don't let anyone tell you what you do isn't important. Of course, writing about pop music ISN'T important, but you can't behave as if that's true. The very best writers fill their pieces with passion, energy and vitality, as if their life depends on every note. If you accept the dirty secret that no one cares, how can you expect to instill that sort of emotion into what you do?

What do you know now that you wish you'd known when you became a music journalist?

I wish I'd known just what it took to be a successful music journalist. I've done okay, but I wish I'd pushed harder to write for more publications when I was younger. I have never been particularly good at pitching ideas to commissioning editors, or motivated enough, and should've spent more time on fixing that. Far too often I see something in a paper and either had the same idea and didn't pitch it, or I didn't spend enough time on the kernel of an idea I had to get it to the same point.

How do you see the future of your profession and what might a young person need to know moving forward?

In 2004, we were constantly told journalists of the future were going to have to know how to do everything and that specialists were a thing of the past. I'd argue that never really came true – not in the one-man-band way predicted – and there is still a place for specialism.

In fact, while so many people can dip into topic areas, it's more important than ever to have an in-depth knowledge. Being able to turn your hand to anything is never going to go out of fashion, and I stand by my advice that Photoshop/video skills are important for young journalists, but knowledge still comes first.

The most successful journalists I know, those really building careers and carving out impeccable reputations, aren't just great writers, but authorities on whatever subject they choose to write about, whether that's an area of music, politics, feminism, film or any other topic. If you're going to write about a subject, own it and read widely.

What's the best thing about your job?

There are several aspects I enjoy – the flexibility of being self-employed and the variety that throws up is about the best. Top of the list is still probably meeting interesting people and getting to ask them as many questions as I want. That was what I thought would be the best thing about my job before I became a journalist and remains true now that I am one.

Tell us about your favourite moments in your job?

This is where I name-drop, right? I am very lucky in that after 12 years as a music journalist, it's easier to list the people I haven't interviewed than those I have. The Rolling Stones (apart from Ronnie Wood), Neil Young, Carole King and Bob Dylan have so far proved elusive, but that's about the same for most music journalists. One of the greatest things is that just when I think I've done it all and spoken to everyone, an opportunity comes along to show me that I haven't.

Going to gigs is great, especially as lots are free, interviewing people is brilliant, or at least can be, but the really special moments come when something hits me and makes me realise how fortunate I've been. I only ever wanted to be a music journalist, and it happened. Hopefully it'll still happen for a few more years yet.

(Interview with author, 2017)

3

INTERVIEWING

There are entire books dedicated to the art of interviewing, and a lot of them are very good. It goes without saying that if you are to be a successful entertainment journalist, it's highly likely that you'll be required to do interviews. The better you are at them, the more successful you'll be. Interviewing people – both 'regular' and celebrities – has been at the heart of my career since I started. Here are some of the things I have learned over that period that will help you.

You

I'm not a particularly confident person and I used to be worse. Among my photos, there is a shot of me with former pop star turned reality personality Kerry Katona and her then husband; I was sweating so profusely that it looks like I just got out of a swimming pool and put clothes on without drying myself. Excessive perspiration was a problem again when it caused me to essentially hide in the corner of a hotel room during a roundtable interview with Hollywood icon Jane Fonda. When I met Mariah Carey – probably the first big star I encountered professionally – she actually asked if I was okay halfway through our chat because I must have looked so terrified. I tell you this not to remind myself of some truly excruciating moments in my personal history, but to tell you not to worry – everyone gets nervous. Carrying out interviews effectively is one of the main things my students come to me with questions or issues about, and a lot of it is down to their own fear. When you're starting out, the idea of meeting and interviewing people, either face-to-face or by phone, can be terrifying. In fact, it *is* terrifying. But you know what? That's not an excuse to avoid it. As Jenny McKay writes in *The Magazines Handbook,*

> Shyness is not necessarily a handicap. Provided it isn't crippling it can even work to your advantage. You are unlikely to irritate your subject by being too

brash if you are shy, and you may even find it easier to establish a rapport as a result.

(McKay, 2013)

One possible way round your timidity is to establish some kind of persona that you use in interviews. Almost like a character who comes out when he or she is talking to people. If you're interviewing for TV or radio (where inhibition is probably less tolerated) and you're going to be seen and/or heard, then there is already a performative aspect at play. Playing up to the camera or mic, if you will. That's not necessarily the case if you're a writer. For me, my most-used interview persona was, basically, Hugh Grant in *Notting Hill*. Remember the bit where he accidentally walks into a press junket and has to interview people he doesn't know while pretending he's from *Horse & Hound* magazine? Let's leave out the fact that sort of happened to me when I did my first press junket in New York for a 2000 film called *Erin Brockovich* and I thought I was just there to speak to Julia Roberts before being ushered into rooms to be confronted by director Steven Soderbergh and co-star Aaron Eckhart, resulting in me hurriedly asking anodyne questions about the plot of the movie. But I'm a middle-class, slightly bumbling, overly apologetic Englishman (remind you of anyone?), and when I've been particularly intimidated by an interviewee, I've found myself almost automatically exaggerating this persona in order to get through my allotted time with a celeb. I've also found that this can lull someone – especially Americans who love a British accent – into a false sense of security. They think they're talking to a bloke who's accidentally wandered into their interview room and is now asking them questions about their personal life, rather than a battle-hardened hack there to get a scoop. I'm not saying it always works, but what it does do is trump any fear I might have of being where I am.

Someone once told me about another excellent method for extracting good material from a famous person: "We asked your fans to send us some questions." It doesn't matter if the questions you've got in your hand were hatched by you and the rest of your office – most famous people are finely attuned to appeasing their supporters. They don't mind giving some adversarial journo the cold shoulder, but it's much harder to refuse to give Caroline from Manchester the information she craves. Yes, this sounds nefarious and maybe it is … a bit, though not as bad as what Sharon Marshall admits to in her memoir *Tabloid Girl*; she writes that she'd often leave an interview after ten minutes, pretending to need a loo break, demonstrating with great flourish to her interviewee that she was turning off her tape recorder and leaving it on the table in front of them. At the same time, she'd leave her bag, with another recorder still running, under the table in order to pick up private conversations when the celebrity thought she was out of the room (Marshall, 2010). I don't advocate that, but if you're scared about trying to extract a difficult news line from a person conditioned by the tabloids and their publicists to say no comment, enlisting the help of 'the audience' can be a useful buffer.

Above all, remember that the more you do it, generally, the less frightening it will be. Nervous energy is always useful; it'll keep your mind sharp. But being overwhelmed tends to go away, and you'll often find the most difficult interviews are the ones with outside pressures rather than any in the room. As McKay writes,

> Once you've met ten mega rock stars, including two of your own heroes, it's easier to face the next one; you know you can do it and you're no longer overawed by the expensive clothes and the entourage of flunkeys or doctors of spin.
>
> *(McKay, 2013)*

Finding a good interviewee

A lot of times you won't have a choice in this. You'll be interviewing someone whose new album is out or an actress up for an award or a soap star with the latest controversial storyline. But you'll also be doing a lot of digging for good people to talk to (see Chapter 1), and there are lots of things to look out for. Primarily, they need to be co-operative. They've got to want to do it. That might take some convincing, but you'd be surprised how many people, in their heart of hearts, are flattered by your approach. They may seem reluctant, but the truth is we all want to be heard, we all believe we're special and have something to say. Your job is to make them realise they should be saying that something to you right now. Ideally they will be articulate. There's a reason the same people appear on television again and again. Yes, part of that is due to laziness on the part of producers. But it's also because if an interviewee demonstrates that they have a grasp on the issue and are eloquent in the way they express that view, it makes journalists' lives a hell of a lot easier.

Credibility and reliability are vital too – are they people your audience will believe, and does their input add to the story rather than take away from its impact? Above all, though, they need to have a connection to the story. That might be directly, in that it happened to them, or it could be a profile about them. But it might also mean that they can offer comment that will elevate the power of your content. What's more, it'll mean that you have something that no one else does. Frequently as a feature writer I could have used Google or cut and paste from existing web resources to complete the articles I was asked to write. By searching someone out to give me that little bit more, it meant that while the story itself may not have been totally original, it was unique because I had new quotes from someone no one else did.

And that's where your inquisitive nature will come in. You have to want to dig deeper than the next person, to find something special in the thing you're creating. When my students argued that they shouldn't be having to include two interviews per article for one of their assignments, I told them that was the difference between them and a non-journalist who might also approach that story. By searching out and acquiring fresh quotes, they were marking themselves out from the hundreds of other content creators who call themselves journalists online and then spend most of their time aggregating other people's work or espousing dull-to-average opinions. "You must have an unquenchable curiosity about everyone and everything to be a good journalist," says McKay. And she adds, "To interview well you must be driven by a desire to question, to find out, to fit together a picture or a narrative from what your subject is saying." (McKay, 2013)

In 2006, I was walking along Santa Monica Boulevard in Los Angeles when, out of the corner of my eye, I caught sight of a poster and more specifically a word, "Volupcity". I loved the sound of it – what on Earth is a Volupcity when it's at home? A non-journalist would have walked on, gone to the diner and read the paper. I stopped, wandered back and saw that it was a club night at a venue for plus-size women. Now my curiosity was firmly piqued. There was a night dedicated to larger women? I started rifling through my mental Rolodex, considering which outlet might be interested in something like this and, as well as that, what the story might be. Cut to a couple of weeks later and I'm standing in the middle of that nightclub in Hollywood trying to find a woman and partner who is half her size for a women's weekly magazine. I grabbed people, asked around, talked to someone called Lushes Thunder, who was great but not quite right, before eventually being pointed in the direction of a dark-haired woman called Goddess Patty, whose boyfriend was the DJ. A professional 'squasher' (don't ask) and intrigued that I was there, Patty agreed to meet me at their house in Long Beach a couple of days later, and it made a great piece.

Perseverance does pay off. I was assigned by teen mag *More* to find a young, female plane crash survivor and eventually, after hours of digging, found myself phoning a cabin in the middle of the Rocky Mountains, where a young lady worked as some kind of park ranger. I'd happened upon a local US newspaper story about a light plane crash in the Rockies a year previously; the pilot had died and his female passenger had been rescued after surviving for several hours in the freezing cold. She was perfect, and I was convinced I had a brilliant story. The phone was handed to her by a colleague, and after I explained why I was calling, she basically told me that she was still suffering too much trauma from the accident to talk to me. I could have pushed it, but I realised she wasn't ready so politely rang off and then sat in my office while I thought about how I was going to find *another* female plane crash survivor. (I did, although it took more hours of searching, and she was a great interview.)

TOBY EARLE – PRESENTER AND WRITER, *LONDON LIVE*

What would you say to a person looking to break into entertainment broadcast journalism right now?

The advancement in technology, platforms and speed of reporting means it is imperative that any journalist has more than the ability to write a feature to a deadline; an understanding of how to use social media as a tool and how to operate a camera to film interviews, as well as editing those rushes, are the skills which are all but expected today. A journalist now must be able to supply a story which can run across multiple platforms and ensure they land on each platform in a way that is tailored to make as large an impact as possible.

This is a competitive industry – you need an arsenal of capabilities to demonstrate that you're versatile, adaptable and prepared to move with emerging consumer demands.

So, that's the dull tech-speak and CV advice.

What you must ask yourself is: "How much do I love this field? How much does film, TV, music and culture play a part in my life?"

Are you in this for glamour? To say to mates down the pub, "This is who I met today …"? If that's why, then toodle-pip. That's not good enough. This industry isn't a dodge, week after week of long lunches or nights out with Jennifer Lawrence, partying till dawn. Time pressure is immense, deadlines line up like end-of-level bosses to obstruct you from making it home, and there's always going to be a story developing just out of your line of sight. It'll land as you log off and are pulling your coat on. Always does.

What you need is a deep and sincere affection for film, TV, music and culture. It has to be stitched into the very fabric of you. Does it annoy you when you see interviews with artists that you want to interview and the questions are so bland that the template they've been printed from is yawning? That has to be a feeling you hold – to want to know more, to want to dig deeper, to want to decipher how art has been made and then be able to relate that to readers or viewers.

What are the three most important things you need as a person working in entertainment television?

1. Find your own voice. Write, write and write some more; blog, vlog or tweet, but practise, practise and then carry on practising. Never stop experimenting with how you write. Think about writers you admire and why you admire them; don't ape them, but consider how they have reached that tone, why it comes so naturally to them. You have a voice – find it.
2. Flexibility – plans will change and whatever you had scheduled is prone to a clash hurling it into the void. Losing your marbles over the canning of a story or being asked to fly out of the door to cover an event is a waste of time. There will be frustrations, and certainly don't be a mug and be taken advantage of, but latching onto those frustrations won't help you hit a deadline. You want to go home at some stage of the day.
3. Be inquisitive – look for a new angle on a story. Don't rehash a tired line.

What do you know now that you wish you'd known when you became an entertainment journalist?

> How much the Internet would drive and transform the industry. I worked on an Internet mag in its early consumer years, but it has accelerated this industry at warp speed. It's as if ten years after the Wright brothers first flew, man stepped on the moon. Technology is an ally – buddy up or else you'll be left behind.

How do you see the future of your profession and what might a young person need to know moving forward?

> As above – embrace technology. Be ready for long stints and to work on stories at first which you might not have dreamt of.

What's the best thing about your job?

> The variety. Speaking to individuals who have shaped or are shaping popular culture, people whose work I respect. Writing scripts for my own TV show and working on live TV. Never knowing what each day might bring. The sort of people who rely on rigid daily structures would be in a spin.

Tell me about your favourite moment in your job?

> I once walked into a room to interview Sir Anthony Hopkins and he started by doing a Tommy Cooper impersonation. My days can be strange.
>
> *(Interview with author, 2017)*

Preparation

I had arrived early and was having a gentle lunch near the venue and getting the questions straight in my head when I realised that I'd forgotten to bring my Dictaphone so I could interview a 1980s pop star turned actor. This was before smartphones had a good recording capacity, so with five minutes before I was supposed to meet him, I had to sprint around the area to find a shop which would sell a suitable device – a job made harder because I was wearing flip-flops – buy it (I only ever ended up using it the once) and then rush to my meeting. I spent the entire discussion completely out of breath and preoccupied, with a nice but slightly confused interviewee. The article I wrote at the end of it was, unsurprisingly, pretty rubbish.

This is just one example of how poor preparation can irreparably damage an interview. What's also true is that doing a bad interview because you haven't prepared properly is utterly infuriating. You look back on it afterwards like a failed date, wondering why you didn't spend just a little bit more time thinking about it or doing some digging.

The comedian Jen Kirkman has a brilliant and thoroughly un-self-pitying article on her website (www.jenkirkman.com) about what parts of an interview she finds annoying. One of them is an interviewer's lack of research and subsequent asking of pointless questions, the answers to which are already well known. Some journalists argue that it's just as important to have the interviewee say the words to them on the record even if they are words we've heard before or aren't ultimately that interesting. It's about the fact they've said it rather than the specifics of what they said. I – and I think Ms Kirkman – would agree that's bunk. "When I do press, usually the person interviewing me has a few weeks lead time," she writes.

> And I get the same questions. Why go into a cool profession where you get to talk to performers and people with something to say or maybe just people who say normal things but in a funny way and then just throw it away with boring crap?
>
> *(Kirkman, 2015)*

What's more, she argues that while she agrees people shouldn't step over the line and ask questions that are impertinent or plain rude, no one seems to take advantage of the fact there is not much "at stake if I say an outrageous thing or give a crazy opinion or let someone in too deep". In other words, sometimes people are ready to truly open up – if only you'd let them.

Kirkman uses the example of being asked about how she started in comedy over and over again. "Unless this is [a comedian's] first interview, the answer is out there," she says.

> It's on Wikipedia and I've talked about it on my podcast and I've answered it in hundreds of interviews all available online. Oh and I wrote about it in my book that came out in 2013. If you only have ten minutes by phone to talk to someone, why waste two of them with this boring question?
>
> *(Kirkman, 2015)*

This is one of the most astute and useful pieces of journalistic advice I've ever read, and it's not even from a journalist. She points to US shock jock Howard Stern (who probably wouldn't classify himself as a hack per se but is nevertheless an incisive and fearless interviewer) as someone who has actually come up with an interesting solution for getting biographical facts out of the way in his interviews by incorporating them into his questions.

Very simply, the more you know the person you're talking to, the better interview you'll do. You can catch people in lies, you can more easily control where you want to go and you'll have a clearer idea of what you want to try and get out of the interviewee. You'll be able to shape the time you have together more specifically if you know that you want to get a particular point or that you have to go through certain things chronologically. It's also much more likely that you'll ask the person a question they've never been asked before, which is always a nice surprise for a celebrity and tends to make for a more engaged interview. You're looking for anecdotes, you're trying to get colour and you need to think about where the interview will sit within the finished content you make (easy if it's a profile). Above all, if you're prepped, you'll be able to take time to think about the answer to the question that you should always ask yourself – "What do *I* want from this interview?"

Finally, make sure you always carry some kind of recording device around with you. If you use it for an interview, always wait until it's recording and then ask if it's okay to record your discussion. Some of you might have learned or be learning shorthand, which is a fantastic skill. But it's hard in a full-on interview scenario to take down quotes properly while you're trying to ask questions and listen to the answers. Eye contact, for one, will be frequently broken. But also, having it on tape will allow you to listen back afterwards, to really dig down into the way someone speaks or the manner in which they answered a specific query. Truman Capote argued that you shouldn't use a recorder as "the moment you introduce a mechanical device into the interview technique, you are creating an atmosphere in which the person isn't going to feel really relaxed, because they're watching themselves" (in Inge, 1987). That is true to an extent and even more so if you're shooting the interview on camera or recording it for radio. But the truth is that if you're in a junket situation, there is already artifice. And personally, while he may have been a brilliant writer, I reckon Capote probably made up a lot of his quotes after the fact. There are ways to be unobtrusive with a recording device, but the very nature of an interview – a conversation taking place for no other reason than you are trying to get information out of the person you are talking to – is inauthentic. Your job is to make the interviewee feel at ease enough to just forget the device is there. Which brings us on to ...

Rapport

This is always one of the hardest things to achieve, particularly in an artificial setting like a junket room if you're interviewing a famous person. The writer and comedian Jane Bussmann recounts hilariously her time as a celebrity interviewer in her memoir *The Worst Date Ever*; she admits hating having to ask rude questions and how she always kept two cast-iron backup questions in her locker for if or when the conversation went a bit awry. She calls them her "Magic Questions". "I'd patented the Magic Questions for interviewing celebrities," she writes. "Magic Celebrity Question One: 'You're in amazing shape, what's your secret?' To which the celebrity always replies, 'Am I? Wow. Thanks. Because I never exercise and live off cheese.'" Her second sure-fire winner? "We all know what you're most famous for, but how does it make you feel when you're not appreciated for your inner talents?" (Bussmann, 2009)

I've always relied on mindless small talk and hope to help build a relationship with my interviewees, especially if they're famous. Softer questions always go first, along with a bit of flattery. Some perceive the experience as a form of platonic flirtation, while *Vanity Fair* writer Marie Brenner calls it "a seduction". According to journalist Frank Banfield,

> An interview is an affair of two. Two brains, two personalities, two points of view come in visible contact, and, just in proportion as this dual play is adequately rendered, is the interview bright and pleasant reading, or dull and lifeless.
>
> *(Cited in Silvester, 1993)*

Remember this attitude goes both ways. I've been flirted with by an interviewee, not because she found me attractive – although at the time I was probably narcissistic enough to think she might have – but as a way to butter me up, so watch out for that.

You do need to think about whether you are making your interviewee believe they are being cared about and listened to. If you are face-to-face, this will be with attentive body language. If it's over the phone, it might be in the understanding or caring tenor of your voice. And listening is vitally important.

In their chapter entitled "Between Investigator and Suspect: The Role of the Working Alliance in Investigative Interviewing" from *Investigative Interviewing* (ed. Bull, 2014) – which is actually a book pertaining to cops talking to potential suspects and victims of crime! – Vanderhallen and Vervaeke (2014) outline a list of building blocks for establishing rapport with an interviewee to get the best outcome. Primary among these is demonstrating empathy, defined as

> an active process of desiring to know the full, present and changing awareness of another person, of reaching out to receive his communication and meaning and of translating his words and signs into experienced meaning and matches at least those aspects of his awareness that are most important to him at the moment.
>
> *(Barrett-Lennard, cited in Vanderhallen and Vervaeke, 2014)*

Others include an informal style of conversation, personalising the interview and 'genuineness' – that is, making the interviewee feel like they are part of an authentic process with someone who is not trying to trick them. But the two Vanderhallen and Vervaeke espouse that are perhaps most important are 'active listening' and how the interviewer holds himself/herself in relation to the person they're talking to. In terms of the latter, that means don't sit too close to one another – a 120-degree angle between participants is optimum (yes, seriously). Active listening is a part of interviewing that even the most well-known interrogators forget – in fact, it's probably worse the more famous the journalist/question-asker becomes and as their ego grows. It's *actually listening to what the person is saying.*

You're almost listening for the pauses in between what someone is saying – for the cues your interviewee is giving you either deliberately or unconsciously which will allow you to probe further or ask a more complex supplementary question. Some of my best quotes have come from me following up an aside which I then latched upon and pursued. As Vanderhallen and Vervaeke write,

> Active listening concerns both nonverbal and verbal behaviour.
>
> [...] Examples of encouragement include nodding, facial expressions ... and the use of such utterances as "hum", "OK" and "I see".
>
> [...] Additional nonverbal activities for engaging in active listening include eye contact and the use of silence to provide the suspect (as well as the interviewer) with time to think.
>
> *(Vanderhallen and Vervaeke, 2014)*

In other words, shut up, let the person speak, hear what they are saying and be interested as they're doing it.

Phoners

A brief further mention of phone interviews here. It's likely that you'll do a lot of these in your career; lack of time and often geographical restrictions will demand it. Bluntly, you're less likely to get such a good response to your questions over the phone. That's because it's harder, if not impossible, to build up a decent rapport, and in these days of smartphones, you might find your interviewee busy doing something else while he or she is also talking to you. So don't let yourself be the one who gets distracted. Think about how you might transpose the methods discussed in the rapport section to this context. And also, use the facilities at your disposal. Be checking facts and answers if you suspect there might be some discrepancies. Make sure the interviewee knows you are listening and engaged with the conversation. Oh – and get yourself a good phone recording device. I use two – microphone-cum-earbuds, which does a good job of recording their audio. But if you are thinking that you might want to put the interview, say, online, after you've edited it, then it might well be worth using Skype and buying software like Call Recorder, which is cheap, deals with sound levels and – if you get yourself a good microphone your end – will also do a good job of picking up your questions as well.

Writing up/editing the interview

My favourite quote about truth and reality in celebrity speak has always belonged to Hollywood producer Robert Evans, who says in his memoir *The Kid Stays In the Picture*, "There are three sides to every story: your side, my side and the truth." (Evans, 1994)

If you're talking to someone for a short amount of time for a news or feature piece, there is no way you're going to fully understand them as people. That's especially true if you're doing a four-minute television junket interview. I don't believe your goal is to do that. My ambition with a celebrity profile is always this – through the research I do and the interview itself, I am trying to make the audience understand what it is like to be the person in question at that specific moment in time. It is a snapshot of them, as textured as I can make it, within the time I have to do it. Whether I have ever achieved that, I don't know. Probably not. And the fast-paced nature of today's journalism means you have even less time to reflect on your encounter and really think about what it meant and how you felt about the person you interviewed. This will be coloured further by the desire not to end your career and the relationship you and/or your company has with the publicist (more on that in Chapter 5 on the PR and Chapter 4 on junkets/red carpets). In other words, there are lots of factors at play here. But it echoes with something celebrity journalist John Powers remembered about his encounter with Al Pacino, which he talked about during a public event at the Norman Lear Centre (Powers, 2002). In the latter stages of the interview, Pacino realised that his fears their discussion was unsuccessful were real, but that it didn't necessarily matter. "He was hopeful, that Powers could find one moment of truth in their hours together, because it's the small things that turn out to be true." So you just have to be as truthful as you can and as clear as you can within the constraints you have. As Powers adds,

> [Celebrities] usually have no interest in revealing their souls to interviewers. Typically, the celebrity creates a persona appropriate for the movie they're promoting, or for their own publicity purposes – something that will fit the narrative arc that their publicists have concocted for them. The journalist must negotiate this terrain with care.
>
> *(Powers, 2002)*

That's a strong statement, but useful to consider. Don't misquote people, though of course there will always be finessing of words to, for instance, get rids of the ums and ahs and ensure sentences make sense. Christopher Silvester quotes Janet Malcolm as saying,

> When a journalist undertakes to quote a subject he has interviewed on tape, he owes it to the subject, no less than the reader, to translate his speech into prose. Only the most uncharitable (or inept) journalist will hold a subject to his literal utterances and fail to perform the sort of editing and rewriting that, in life, our ear automatically and instantaneously performs.
>
> *(Cited in Silvester, 1993)*

She called it "fidelity to the subject's thought" – I call it not screwing anyone over.

Should you be in the story? Almost certainly not. At least, not unless you're (a) famous yourself or (b) that's house style or (c) something happened to you during the process of the interview that you being in it is fundamental to the narrative.

Otherwise, it's best to remind yourself that you're not the story. People don't care what you think; they care what the interviewee thinks. Of course, this won't matter if your interview is simply part of the tapestry of the content you've created, an expert to clarify a point perhaps, rather than the crux of it. If that's the case, then try not to cram your content full of multitudinous viewpoints – articles with quote after quote after quote look messy – but utilise them sparingly and effectively. Be prepared too to kill your darlings. In this instance, that means the amazingly hilarious 300-word anecdote about getting lost on the way to Inverness in a camper van with a dog and one rasher of bacon gets cut. You don't have the word count or length of video to do it justice, and also, like trouser pockets bearing a bulky wallet and phone do to your silhouette, it damages the 'line' of your story.

Ten top tips – interviewing

1. Remember that interviewing is a form of performance. That's particularly true if you're doing it for broadcast of course, but even if you're not, you need to understand there's always some acting involved.
2. Being a good interviewer and enjoying the process of finding and talking to people is absolutely fundamental to this job. If you don't like it or don't want to do it, find a different career.
3. The people you get to meet and talk to as an entertainment journalist will be amongst the most fascinating you'll ever encounter. Revel in it.
4. You'll never truly know the person you're talking to. If I'm writing a profile, my take on it is that I'm creating a snapshot of a person in that moment based on my observations and informed by the research I've done leading up to our meeting.
5. Interviewees are not your friends. You can have a benevolent relationship with them, but the moment you think you're friends is when you find the rug pulled from under you. Meeting celebrities, it's very easy to get suckered in by their charisma, only realising later that you've been played. Be careful.
6. Try and come up with one question you think they've never been asked. Believe me, coming up with one is really difficult.
7. The more you prepare, the better the interview will be.
8. Try and avoid asking questions you already know the answer to.
9. If you've got a difficult question to ask, come up with multiple ways of asking it beforehand. It's likely they'll try and deflect it, so having another way in can be useful.
10. If you're interviewing more than one person at the same time, make sure you ask questions to specific people. Otherwise you can end up with a series of messy answers, or the person you really want to speak stays quiet while the less interesting person does all the talking (for example, a director/producer and star teamed up for a junket interview). If you're recording them for a print interview, it also means you aren't left panicking about who said what on the audio file.

HANNAH HARGRAVE – CELEBRITY AND ENTERTAINMENT NEWS JOURNALIST FOR *US WEEKLY* AND OTHERS

What are the three most important things you need as an entertainment news journalist?

1. The ability to take a current news or celebrity story and create a new lead. A hot story generally won't be very hot for long, but if you can find another angle quickly, you can make and sell a story while it's still current.
2. A thick skin! You have to make a lot of calls, door knocks and introductions to people who often don't want to talk to you. Sometimes you can feel like a cold call sales person, with the phone being put down on you or a door being shut in your face. Also some editors can be very harsh. If they don't like your work, they'll tell you – and not always in a very nice way.
3. Speed. News moves on quickly. You have to be able to produce content swiftly, before it's no longer news.

What do you know now that you wish you'd known when you became an entertainment and news journalist?

Just how hard the grind is. While I love making my own schedule, it's definitely a rollercoaster ride being freelance. Some months there's a ton of work and others it's like everyone has shut up shop. But then this is the case with any freelance work.

At least there's always news happening. Sometimes you just have to be more creative to make money from it.

How do you see the future of your profession and what might a young person need to know moving forward?

It's all going digital. If you want a career that will go the distance, don't just focus on writing magazine/website articles. Learn the art of building a website and using a CMS. If you have that online knowledge, it will broaden your career horizons no end.

What's the best thing about your job?

I've travelled extensively across America for my work, and before I had children, I could wake up in California and go to bed in Hawaii. The excitement of having a new story every day keeps the job fresh, and I got to see and speak to some very interesting people in the process.

Tell us about your favourite moments in your job?

There have been many. Attending the Golden Globes in 2016 was a fantastic moment. I'd only ever been on the other side of the red carpet, so to mingle with the stars as opposed to just interviewing them was a brilliant opportunity.

Then this is a little bizarre, but I once flew all the way to Kalamazoo to knock on Verne Troyer's parents' door. He was in Celebrity Big Brother at the time. Quite often in these cases the address would be wrong or they'd just have a few lines to say. But this time they not only invited me in, but they opened up all their family albums, regaled stories of him hiding in a washing machine and dressing as Little Bo Peep. They then invited me to ride his quad bike and come and spend the summer in Verne's bed when he was away. I didn't go, but they were some of the sweetest people I ever met.

I covered Michael Jackson's molestation court case. It was manic, doing shifts with other journalists inside the courthouse. Although I was panicked I wouldn't be able to get ALL the details down, it was definitely a rush to be covering such a huge news story.

And I love any time one of my stories made the front page, as well as the extensive travelling I've done. It's not just the obvious places like Hawaii and the Bahamas that have been amazing. It's the small towns that I never knew existed too.

(Interview with author, 2017)

4

JUNKETS AND RED CARPETS

I've done *a lot* of press junkets. Tom Cruise and I? We go way back. Having a chat with Daniel Craig about his shoes? Tick. I've spent a huge part of my career talking to famous people in hotel rooms around the world, and for the most part it's been pretty fun (more on when it wasn't and why later). I've probably done even more red carpet events. Some have been amazing, like getting dressed up in a tuxedo and standing in the sunshine at the Oscars or getting invited to the backstage parties for the Golden Globes and getting mistaken for a famous actress' boyfriend (the closest I've ever got to actually dating a celebrity). Others had me standing outside a new London club launch waiting to chat someone who once did a sex tape with Katie Price, while my cameraman stuffed his face with canapés. Either way, both of these experiences are a fundamental part of an entertainment journalist's life and an important method for getting stories.

What is a junket?

At the risk of sounding like a wedding speech, the Merriam-Webster dictionary describes a junket as "a promotional trip made at another's expense". This is essentially true, although the trip can be very short – down the road to a local hotel, for example. When people talk of movie junkets, they speak of lavishly funded five-star trips to the Bahamas to speak to the teenage star of a new comedy, or a weekend in Barcelona in order to extract a few words from a recent Oscar winner. And plenty of these do exist. I live in the UK and was recently invited on a visit to a movie set in Boston. I've run lines with actors in a swimming pool in Athens during a three-day jaunt in which I did a maximum of half-an-hour of actual work. I've talked to Sylvester Stallone next to a Caesars Palace boxing ring in Las Vegas. Each year for the past decade or so, one film company has flown a slew of journalists to a luxury Mexican resort in order to introduce them to the stars and creators of their latest film slate. Hurricane warnings aside, it was pretty awesome.

But for the most part, that's not the reality of a press junket. The reality of a press junket is making your way to a hotel in the city where you live, where you are herded into an anteroom and forced to wait for sometimes hours while the 'talent' speaks to a hundred other journalists before you. I'm not saying it's like mining for coal, but after the first couple of times, when you're embarrassedly blasé to the opulence, or even mildly angry that real people have enough money to live in such a way, it's far more mundane. Primarily this is because you are the least important person there. Yes, you've come to help the celebrity promote whatever they're promoting, but so have a load of other people – and the star's family, hangers-on, agent, etc. come before you in the pecking order. The skill for you here is to acknowledge that and figure out how you're still going to get something authentic and fun out of your experience which will make for a good story on your outlet. Junkets in one form or another will be the primary artery by which you have access to the people your audience loves and wants to hear from, so it behoves you to make them count.

Junket etiquette

Don't whinge. Yes, you're bored; yes, so-and-so just got here and went in before you. We can hear the world's smallest violin playing. I once waited over two hours for Mariah Carey to be ready to receive me at a London hotel, and by the time I finally sat down with her, I had cycled through all the emotions from terror to rage to ennui back to fury and then complete passivity. By the time I actually got to speak to Ms Carey, my concentration was shot and I did a mediocre job (not helped by being surrounded by television cameras and about 30 members of her entourage). This is the job. Get over it.

Make sure you turn up in plenty of time. The publicists will secretly love you for it and you can always relax while you wait. It might mean that you get sneaked in early as well.

If you're doing a filmed junket – that is one with cameras already set up for you – then listen to the people who are operating them and/or telling you how much time you have left in your interview. I should probably take a moment here to explain this a bit further. If you're doing the junket for a print or audio piece, then the likelihood is you'll be brought into a room with the star, told you have a certain amount of time (it can range from three minutes – seriously! – to whenever, but normally no more than an hour at an absolute maximum in a junket setting), then left to your own devices, with maybe a publicist piping up when you have one question left. If you're representing a video outlet, it's a little different. For a lesser name, you might have brought your own equipment, and then the set-up would be similar to print/audio. But there are also junkets in which a camera company has been employed to provide a set-up for you. These are the kinds you see on TV and social media all the time – a movie star with the poster for their film in the background doing an impression of their fellow actor or explaining how this will be the last episode in the franchise, honest. A small number of companies dominate this field of video work, and you'll see them at multiple junkets throughout the year (I once even bumped into a couple of them while in Rome).

As a journalist, you'll walk into a specially lit room with two cameras set up to capture both the celebrity and you, with microphones hanging over your seat and the star sitting in front of you. Depending on the magnitude of your interviewee, it can be pretty daunting, and it's likely they will have been talking to a lot of people for a number of hours before you. You know your job and you can try to focus on that, but you'll need to listen out for the other most important person in that room who is the one timing your interview. They tend to sit on the periphery of your eyeline and will hold up fingers as the clock counts down, telling you how long you've got. When it's time to wrap up, they'll swirl their finger about and start shuffling, signalling you better shut up and get the hell out of there because they've got another four hundred interviewers to come and the celeb wants his pastrami and kale sandwich. Which is why I suggest always asking a really open question as your final one rather than the classic "So what are you up to next?" If it's something you know they really want to talk about, then you'll be able to eke some extra time out of your slot – the timing guru will never shut down the interviewee, only you.

Remember that you're not there as a fan. You may love the person you're talking to or the show you're there to talk about. And that's brilliant – it means you'll bring an added dimension of insight to your questions, and you'll be generally more upbeat about the process because you're excited to be there. This can also cause problems. One of my first-ever interviews when I was at university was with a long-defunct Britpop band who I adored. I spent most of our allotted time for the student newspaper asking the lead singer/songwriter what the chords were for my favourite song on their album. I learned how to play the tune, but I didn't have much actual content for my feature. So be aware that you're trying to speak as a member of your audience – think about what they want to know and what might be most interesting to them. In a junket situation, this fan-worshipping can also manifest itself in much more embarrassing ways that will make you seem extremely amateurish. Asking your interviewees to sign stuff at the end of the interview comes under this heading. This used to happen a lot when I lived in Los Angeles and it always infuriated me. It's not only that it delays everything – you're there as a journalist. Once when I was doing a roundtable interview with Quentin Tarantino, a fellow writer pulled about ten DVDs out of his rucksack and proceeded to ask the writer/director to sign all of them. I couldn't quite understand why he agreed – it seemed perfectly clear to me that the journalist was going to flog them all on Ebay, not admire them in his home library. I lost all respect for that reporter then. Similarly, back when I started, it was considered a cardinal sin to ask the celeb to pose for a picture or do a shout-out. I know that's changed in recent years with the advent of social media and the increase in selfie culture. Sometimes editors ask that you get a picture with the person you're talking to so that you can put it on Twitter. I still cringe if I have to do this and it feels very unprofessional to me, but it's a more accepted practice these days. Personally, I don't know why anyone bothers. Did it not happen if there's not a picture to commemorate it? Isn't a picture basically a humblebrag to say look at me, aren't I great, I'm hanging out with so-and-so? To me, that's what it seems like. Focus on the experience itself and concentrate on what you have to achieve there rather than worrying about how many likes you'll get later on Facebook.

Lots of people have asked me about what to wear for a junket. If you're on camera, then this is a no-brainer – some well-known presenters doing a junket will bring their own make-up artists to the hotel to make them look fabulous. I've been (jokingly, I think) chastised by an A-list movie star for my decrepit, unironed T-shirt and trousers ensemble when I met her ("Thanks for dressing up for me" was her opening comment after I'd introduced myself). The answer is probably somewhere in the middle. Be smart enough that you look like you know what you're doing and care about being there. This is harder when you're in a boiling-hot room in the middle of the desert when the air conditioning has been turned off because it's too noisy, or when you're at the Sundance Film Festival and you're conducting an interview in a hastily constructed tent near the main drag with a temperature of minus two degrees Celsius outside. But you don't need to rent a tux or anything.

NDAs. Now, NDAs, short for non-disclosure agreements, are the bane of many junketeers' lives. According to British editor Emma Soames, "The star system, led by Hollywood, has hijacked the interview, tied it up and all but killed it stone dead. ... Interviewees – admittedly only if they are rich or famous – now control the interview." (Quoted in Silvester, 1993) Thanks to the rise of social media and blog-style reporting, I don't think it's necessarily as bad as she makes out. However, the use of NDAs have expanded and contracted over the years. Essentially they are embargo documents – which you're often told you must sign before participating in a junket – outlining when you can post/publish/broadcast the material you accrue. This is particularly prevalent in the social media era since the carefully curated release strategy of a movie studio/music company/TV channel is constantly under threat from Internet spoilers. However, these NDAs have grown in scope to include everything from where you may or may not place material (as a freelancer I've been banished from particular parts of a junket because, for example, a female star's publicist was worried I would sell a feature to a men's magazine with, say, a screen grab of an on-screen nude scene an actress might have done, even though I would never do such a thing) or even the kinds of questions you may ask the person you're interviewing. It's the latter point that many journalists find difficult to stomach. Mainly because the banned areas of inquiry generally revolve around the parts of the person's life that have the most potential story value. But in terms of etiquette, the line is pretty clear here. If you don't want to abide by the NDA, don't do the junket. If you sign the document but then turn around and go back on it later, it seems dishonest and idiotic. It'll come back to bite you in the form of blackballing or restricted access. Yes, it would be much better if there were no such things as NDAs and the stars were considered grown-up enough to refuse to answer a question politely if it's posed to them, like in any normal person's conversation. After all, they're not stupid (at least most of them aren't) – they know what people are interested in asking them. But because of the promotional ecosystems around them now, that's no longer the case. Sometimes, in fact, these restrictions are put in place by their PR team purely to justify the thousands the star is spending on them. That's frustrating for sure, but if you've signed the contract, then don't be unprofessional and ignore it.

Be respectful – though not totally deferential – of the process. Everyone there, however false the structure, is just trying to do their job. Make it easy for them to do so. This extends to the other journalists. There are people on the circuit who have never asked a question in a group (roundtable) interview. They just sit there, recording everyone else's hard work before writing it up as their own for their outlet. Don't be one of these journalists. Come up with interesting questions, not just for the biggest star on the junket, but the others too. I once did a junket for a film starring Catherine Zeta-Jones in a room full of about 20 hacks from around the world. When the actress sat down, every journalist shouted out questions (mostly related to when Ms Zeta-Jones was going to next visit their country) for the 15 minutes she was in the room. A few moments later, her co-star was brought in and those same journalists buried their heads in their notebooks and didn't say a word. It was embarrassing and unprofessional. Yes, you might never use that material, but at least show some respect. You never know when one of the supporting players that you thought was inconsequential at the time turns out to be massive. Early in my career I was sent to get a Guy Pearce interview for his latest movie. One of the other actors doing the junket was a posh, young British kid called Henry Cavill. He wasn't media-trained at that point and said some funny things that I could probably turn into a feature now, but I threw the tape away long ago. Dumb.

How to get the best out of a junket

- *Listen to the people around you.* There's always a lot of people milling around a junket. Listen to what they're saying. They'll be talking about the mood of the stars, whether they're ahead or behind time (99% of the time they'll be behind) or what silly questions people asked ... as a journalist, you should always try and be the most informed person in the room. By keeping your ears open in a junket, you might get that extra nugget of useful material that will help you do a better job.
- *Get on the PRs' good sides.* There's a whole chapter on this coming up next, but a good relationship with the PRs at a junket is imperative. If they like you, they'll stump for you in front of the interviewee's people; they'll try and make the experience better for you. There's always this sense that the relationship between hacks and flacks must by design be adversarial. I don't believe that's

the case. If nothing else, they know more about the intimate details of the situation than you do and are thus perfectly placed to give you tips. There's nothing better than an indiscreet publicist in full flow. I remember a great conversation in the Los Angeles Four Seasons Hotel in which a PR complained loudly to me about how they had to disrupt a private plane ride from Hollywood to New York by going via Texas so the famous person she was accompanying could visit his preferred home-town marijuana dealer and stock up. I was too nice to do anything with the information at the time – even though I'm sure I could have sold it to an American tabloid – but it makes for a good anecdote!

- *Get on the camerapeople's good side if you're doing a filmed junket.* The people running the cameras are the gatekeepers. They will be the ones who shut off the camera if you slightly overrun your interview. They will be the ones who delay, waggling their finger just a few moments so you can get out that important final question. If you're on camera, they will make you look presentable!

- *Don't try to make friends with the talent.* This is a total waste of your time. You are the four hundredth person they've spoken to that day; they're jet-lagged and probably went out on the town the night before seeing as it's all being paid for by the film company/music label/channel. This is a transaction to them – it's what they're paid the big bucks for. That can make it sound depressing, but it's not supposed to. It's no different to an investigative journalist interviewing a politician – you're there to get answers to the questions you have, not invite them to your house for a cup of tea. This dynamic alters slightly when journalists are talking to stars, because of the way our brains react to fame. But I've talked to lots of lots of famous people and I'd say that with 99.9% of them, I could care less whether they'd be my friend. Trust me, your mates are far more interesting and funny and cool. The most astute stars will act like politicians and might remember your name or, at least, act like they do. Will Smith is famously loved by the international press because he has embraced every German, French and Taiwanese journo like they were his best buddy. When I interviewed the actor Tom Sizemore (*Saving Private Ryan*), he got up from his seat when I walked into the room and enthusiastically talked about how he remembered me. I told him, rather confused, that we've never met before. He laughed, apologised and admitted that he said that to every journalist he meets because it makes them feel good before they start his interview.

- *Ask questions; don't make statements.* You don't get very long in a junket. If it's filmed, you might get an outside chance at eight minutes, but that's usually a double slot. If you're doing it for print, you'll often be in a roundtable scenario where you're sharing your time with five or more other journalists who want to ask their, often country-specific, questions too. Even if you've managed to wangle a one-on-one with someone, unless you work for a top broadsheet newspaper or magazine, it's often unlikely you'll get more than 20 minutes. So be pithy. Know what you want to ask and ask it. Similar to my point above, keep the pleasantries to a minimum – while still trying to establish rapport as discussed in Chapter 3 – and be direct. When interviewers meet someone, they often want to demonstrate how much they understood the subtext of the product that's being promoted, or how their theory about a songwriter's lyrics being a cipher for the difficult relationship he had with his colleague while working as a teenager at a canning factory is, like, totally correct. Get over yourself. This isn't about you. You don't have time to make it be about you. Ask the questions.

- *Don't be afraid to interrupt.* People blather on for all kinds of reasons. They're boring, they're self-absorbed, they're obfuscating and attempting to pivot away from the question you've asked and back onto something they're comfortable talking about. Junket interviews are littered with unusable two-minute answers about how such-and-such loved working with so-and-so because they're incredibly talented, followed by three interesting answers hurriedly spat out in the course of another minute. I'm not saying be rude, but boss the interview. There are ways to break into someone's spiel and get on with it. Yes, they're famous; yes, they can be intimidating – but you'll regret it if you don't.

- *Take other work with you.* You'll spend a lot of time in those hotel anterooms. Don't waste the time. Use it to finish up other work. Or take the book you never get around to reading.

- *Make friends.* I've made some of my best work friends through doing junkets together. If you get onto the circuit, you'll see the same people all the time. There can be a tendency in some journalism circles to get competitive, to treat fellow hacks like they're out to steal your thunder. Yes, they're looking for a good story too. But if you're an intelligent journalist, you'll have found a way to get something good out of your interviewee that no one else will have – unless they've copied your notes. I'm still friends with many of the people I met doing junkets; in fact, several of them have contributed to this book. They'll make you better at your job, make you enjoy it, and you'll laugh a lot together too. Plus, if you're like me, there'll be photographic evidence of big nights out where you can't quite remember how you got home. And of course, it's great networking too. One of these friends pointed out a great tip in this vein as well – when you leave any junket, jot down the names and maybe a bit of information about the people you met into your phone's notes. Unless you're one of those freaky people who can remember everyone's name and every-thing about them, it's always useful to have a record, especially regarding publicists, crew and the assorted hangers-on who always seem to be at every junket. As I've said, you'll see a lot of the same people around. If you have something to talk to them about, it'll put you in good stead for favours and advantages.

- *Keep an eye on your time.* Make sure you know how long you have to talk. Make sure you've thought about how to structure your interview so you can get through all the points that you want to cover. And if you're working with video, get good at seeing the timekeeper's fingers doing their countdown business out of the corner of your eye while still maintaining eye contact and concentrating on your subject.

- *Ask about the product first.* No one really wants to chat about the boring generic details of the product the celebrity is selling. But you need to at least acknowledge that you recognise it's why you've been invited here in the first place. Get one or two questions out of the way initially and then get to the good stuff.

Five junket scenarios I encountered and what I learned from them

1. John Cusack/Billy Crystal – neither Cusack nor Crystal wanted to speak to me. The former ignored me for the majority of the short time I had with him, and the latter had a baseball game showing on the TV in the corner of his room and was far more interested in that than answering my questions. This isn't intended to be a chance to criticise them – they had their reasons. But what those experiences made me realise is not to be beholden to the people I was interviewing. I didn't interview Cusack during the height of his popularity (I was a big fan) and the film he was promoting was an anodyne romcom. So I didn't need to waste my time if he wasn't going to engage. So after about a minute of non-answers, I said thank you very much and walked out. (FYI, about ten years later I interviewed him again and he was much more amenable – I blame the rubbish film for the first instance.) The same could be said of Billy Crystal. Again, I like a lot of movies he's been in, but when I talked to him, it was for an animated voice-over and he wasn't the story.

2. Russell Crowe – anyone who's ever interviewed Russell Crowe will have a story to tell about it. He's, shall we say, a challenge for journalists. I interviewed him in Rome for his Oscar-winning film *Gladiator*. A colleague had been sworn at during his previous junket. When I walked into the room – having been flown to Italy specifically to get something good from this five-minute chat – he was smoking. I couldn't have someone using a cigarette on camera. When I asked him to put it out, he picked up the packet and held it up to the camera, asking me to start the interview. I called his bluff – didn't back down or get intimidated – and asked my first question. He was a delight from then onwards. I demonstrated to him that he couldn't push me about, and I think he respected that. Don't be afraid to act in the same way if a celebrity is proving difficult.

3. An unnamed indie director – fell asleep during my interview with him. Luckily, it was for a film no one really cared about, and we were only doing the junket as a favour to someone. Yet it seriously dented my confidence. I was told it was because of jet lag (he sort of fell asleep and then woke himself up a few seconds later), but be aware that there are lots of things going on behind the scenes at junkets that you are not privy to. Regardless of what's happened on the tour so far or during that day, you only get to

walk into an interview set-up and ask someone questions,. I've ruined interviews for other people by asking a stupid question to a star and making them annoyed for the rest of the day. I've also made the next person's interview a better experience by doing the same thing, because the actor in question was so pleased to be rid of me. I've witnessed an actor's harem walking round a luxury hotel, and I've talked to couples who had a hot fling on set and had broken up by the time it came to promote the movie. As a journalist, there's no way to control all of that stuff. You can only deal with what's put in front of you.

4. Tyra Banks – I met the former supermodel on one of my earliest international junkets, when she was still dabbling in acting. It'd been the premiere the night before, and all the travelling journalists had been invited to the after-party. Being young and excitable, I'd overindulged and acted pretty stupidly. Tyra greeted me the next morning by saying, "Oh yeah, you were the guy dancing with David Hasselhoff." I resolved to never be as (publicly) unprofessional again.

5. Professor Brian Cox – I secured a phone interview with the TV physicist as part of his marketing blitz for his first big TV show, *Wonders of the Solar System*. I'm useless at science and had never heard of him, and even though he was willing to talk and I could have had lots of time with him, I did a rudimentary job. I filed the piece and thought nothing of it. Two years later, I got a phone call from a publishing company asking me to write a biography of him. If I'd been a bit more thorough and a bit more thoughtful about that initial interview, I would have had much more personal material that I could have fed into the book. I didn't – and I've always regretted it. Put in the effort, even if the interview doesn't seem like a big deal at the time. You never know when it will come in useful.

SOPHIA MOIR – TV EDITOR, METRO.CO.UK

What would you say to a person looking to break into your profession right now?

> It will take time – don't expect it to come easily. The worst mistake I made out of uni was thinking that I'd walk straight into a graduate job. It can take years before someone believes in you and offers you that first job.

What are the three most important things you need as an online entertainment journalist?

1. Knowledge of popular culture. It's not enough just to come into work and assume you know enough about the topic you're writing about – you have to be up to date with what's going on in the world. For example, at MTV we were expected to know what's going on in the world of TV and our

competitors, but at a minimum you should also read up on daily world news/politics.

2. Flexibility. Online journalism is a relatively new industry compared to print and broadcast, so you're expected to have a broad set of skills – writing breaking news, using social media and doing video editing, to name a few. Brush up on and practice these skills as soon as you can.

3. A thick skin. You'll come across a lot of people who have been in the business a long time who think they know everything and aren't prepared to listen to what anyone else has to say. Learn to accept that nothing is personal and nothing is worth taking home with you at the end of the day. Brush it off and move on.

What do you know now that you wish you'd known when you became an online journalist?

It's a very insecure industry and people move around a LOT. There are few permanent jobs around; most are temporary/contract/shift work. You have to really love it, because you'll probably be working unsociable hours.

How do you see the future of your profession and what might a young person need to know moving forward?

More jobs merging into the world of marketing – a lot of this is already happening (online journalists doing social media marketing/marketers doing online journalism). I'd advise people to scratch up on their social media marketing skills and immerse themselves in new social media technologies and apps.

What's the best thing about your job?

The people – everyone is young, hungry to learn, like-minded and passionate.

Tell us about your favourite moment in your job?

Being responsible for the best day of traffic the MTV UK website has ever seen – and everyone knowing about it! (Nobody has beaten it since ...)
(Interview with author, 2017)

What is a red carpet event?

For me, a red carpet event is any kind of public premiere or launch to which the press is invited and people involved in the project offer themselves up to be questioned about it. As I mention above – the range of these events can be huge. It could be a gigantic Leicester Square extravaganza with extras dressed up as characters from the movie, or it could be a parade of potential awards recipients and cinematic icons waiting to see who's been deemed the best of the year. It could also be a tiny strip of material outside a club or a shop, the only attendees a wannabe boy band or a couple of minor reality show participants. Neither is necessarily better than the other from a journalistic perspective. At a super-shiny blockbuster premiere, you might get a slew of boring answers along with some nice pictures, which are what you rely on to make it a readable story the next day. Alternatively, there might be someone who shows up at the less desirable event and then says something newsworthy in a desperate and transparent attempt to make a splash. As a reporter, that's the one you want. As Holly Forrest writes in *Confessions of a Showbiz Reporter*, "The majority [of premieres] don't get the kind of blanket national press coverage that publicists dream of. But when they work, they *really* work." (Forrest, 2013)

How to succeed on a red carpet

Be prepared to wait – and take a coat. Press accreditation always happens early on red carpets, meaning you have to show up well before the people you're going to interview. At the Oscars, you're expected to be there at midday, and the celebrities don't start arriving until 3 p.m. at the earliest. Yes, it's dull, but you should also use the time to get your B roll (illustrative shots of the event to edit into your piece) if you're filming it and to prepare your questions. But make sure you check the weather forecast before you go. If it suddenly starts getting nippy, you probably won't be able to go away and get a coat. And if it begins to rain? Follow the Scout motto.

Have your questions ready to go at any moment. Working the red carpet is like being an elite sportsman in that success can come down to a few seconds. I've watched fellow journos flannel about while a celeb stands in front of them, unable to ask a question because they're unprepared. When I interviewed Tom Cruise at a premiere, I got star-struck – about the only time I think – and completely lost my train of thought because I didn't think I'd get to speak to him. He stood smiling in front of me while I told him not to leave and reached around my addled brain trying to come up with something good. I didn't.

Don't act like you're better than the other people on the line. Inevitably, there's a pecking order on the red carpet. When you arrive, there are little signs saying where you'll be standing. At the Cruise premiere, I was 79th in line (I still remember!), at the Academy Awards, even further down. That doesn't necessarily matter (see the section on Baz Bamingboye at the Oscars in Chapter 1), and it's cheap and petty to lord it over the people you're above. Mainly because they'll probably be ahead of you the next time around.

Keep checking your phone for breaking news. With a premiere, you're always looking for a fresh angle on questions. "What are you wearing?" or "Do you think you'll win?" only work in certain circumstances. The red carpet isn't really a place to go into a nuanced argument either. If something happens – and you know about it because you're on top of current affairs – it's potentially an issue you can ask the people you're interviewing about. It'll give you a much better story than where they'll put their BAFTA.

Don't hog the stars. This is an etiquette thing. As a red carpet reporter, I always thought you should ask a maximum of four questions. This sounds arbitrary and totally is. But nothing infuriated me more than an outlet monopolising what is already a short amount of time to ask a slew of questions when they know that whatever they get will be edited down to a maximum of 30 seconds. Be aware of those below you in the line. Understand where you are. And if you're not a good enough journalist to get what you need after four questions, you don't deserve to be there.

Interview the little people. Red carpet events are where anyone desperate for fame spies an opportunity to get some airtime, primarily because there tends to be a lot of photographers present. Your editor may have asked you to make sure you get a few quotes from a certain Brit Award-winning singer, but it's also worth speaking to the lesser names before the main event shows up. Not only will it get you in the interview groove but it'll also endear you to the PRs, who next time will bring one of their bigger clients for a chat. Plus, in the age of digital, you aren't going to be wasting any resources.

Make sure you have access to Wi-Fi. This is more for those who are having to live tweet an event. It's worth speaking to the organisers beforehand to check that you're not in a black spot; if in doubt, get the password of the restaurant next door to the venue (shhhh).

It tends to be worth staying those extra few moments. One gets a feel for when an event is winding down, but make sure you get the official word. Sometimes there'll be a late arrival, or one of the stars will come out of the cinema and head back to the car before the movie actually begins and you'll have an opportunity to talk to them without the other press screaming for their attention alongside you. Good journalism doesn't happen easily. It's about time and graft. Don't ever forget that, especially when you're easing your feet into a hot bath after standing for ten hours at an awards show.

On that note, and like at junkets, listen for developments. There'll be rumours that one person isn't showing up or that someone else will be coming in the side entrance rather than on the red carpet itself. Being open to that kind of intel could give you the edge.

Working with a cameraperson

If you're doing the event for video, you'll generally be working with a camera-person. Yes, sometimes you'll be doing it by yourself, but I'd urge you to get someone else from the office to come with you, even if they don't know one end of the camera from the other. Equipment these days is pretty idiot-proof anyway, and it's important that someone else can check that your carefully planned shot hasn't gone out of focus because the person next to you accidentally trod on the tripod. The relationship you have with your cameraperson at a premiere is crucial. Let them guide you in terms of where to stand and be aware of any pokes or prods you might get mid-interview. That probably means that you've pushed your head or hand into shot or are holding the microphone too close to the interviewees' mouths. Make sure you've got plenty of B roll before you start your interviews and that the cameraperson continues to get plenty while the event is going on. And be space aware. It doesn't happen quite so much these days with smaller cameras, but they hurt when they bash into you. I always remember a colleague telling me about the shame of clocking a celebrity in the head with the camera battery when the operator turned to get some footage in the opposite direction. I saw the female celebrity in question cradling her bonce after the incident happened. But there are some best practices and mistakes that only a cameraperson can spot. I asked former entertainment cameraman Ben Robinson to reveal good and bad experiences:

> Good – Journalists who knew their story and did their research. Where possible, they created an editorial format early into the shoot or shaped the story rapidly so they could direct me to get appropriate coverage/B roll.
>
> Bad – We interviewed the wrong person, or the story was too vague and unfocused and so was never aired. They clearly hadn't cleared it with their senior producers – a huge waste of time.
>
> Good – Their interview technique was sharp and perceptive. They had done research and created rapport with the interviewee, which meant people opened up.
>
> Bad – I have been kicked off a movie set because producers asked silly or flippant questions. On one occasion we were on the Isle of Man and were kicked out and had to go back to London with no story because the producer was cocky or trying to be funny.

Five things to watch out for at a red carpet event

1. *That boy band who is always just ... there.* As I said above, there are always people ready to come to premiere events, especially at the start of their career when they're trying to get traction with the press. At every premiere, there will always be a fresh-faced band you've never heard of – even if you're a pop music expert – who bounds up to you talking about how their songs are amazing, how excited they are to be there and who their celebrity crush is. It's worth speaking to them, the first time anyway. You never know, they might be the next One Direction.

2. *There always seems to be loads of children at premieres.* Mostly they're kids of the stars, getting a chance to put on their party gear and share the limelight with mum or dad. But sometimes they're child actors, again, told to tread the red carpet by a wily publicist to make them seem more important than they are. If you avoid anyone at premieres, avoid youngsters. Unless they are already

big, they're generally boring to talk to and you can't ask them any interesting questions anyway.

3. *Focus on the people you want to talk to.* I once watched some hilarious footage of our Hollywood correspondent talking happily to the lead in a successful teen-centric TV show when a more famous movie star walked behind him on the carpet. The reporter apologised and launched his arm across the telly guy, shouting the movie actress' name while the first guy stood embarrassedly looking into the camera. You want to try and avoid this. Once the event gets going, there's generally a constant stream of celebs walking a carpet, and you might be faced with the arrival of someone you actually want to talk to when you're conversing with someone you could take or leave. Be aware of it and try not to be rude. Get good at wrapping up interviews quickly. Or a better method is welcoming the second celeb into your current interview, introducing them to the person you're with (if they don't know them) and conducting a kind of joint interview.

4. *You've got to have elastic arms.* Yes, you'll be doing a lot of interviewing yourself, but one of the good things about premieres is that you can always sneak your mic into others. And occasionally, if you've got a poor position on the carpet, you'll have to do some arm gymnastics to get any kind of useable quote. There are paparazzi pictures of premieres I've been to where all you can see are my fingers reaching out into the small nook between one person's head and another's shoulder to try and record something. This is also why it's good to make friends with the people who are standing around you. Countless times I've helped fellow journalists get a quote on the red carpet by holding someone else's microphone, and the favour has often been repaid.

5. *And, finally, remember you're there to work.* "Once the curtains go up, we have to go straight back to work," writes Holly Forrest. "When the final celebrity has arrived, the final flashbulb has popped, the final interview wound up, it's back to the office we go to write up the night's events." (Forrest, 2013)

Ten top tips – red carpets (Courtesy of Colin Paterson)

Because we've already covered interviewing, I'm going to focus here purely on red carpets. And for this, I'm going to turn once again to red carpet reporter extraordinaire, the BBC's Colin Paterson (whose expert interview is featured at the end of this chapter), who has given us ten brilliant tips for working a premiere-style showbiz event.

1. Think about the wider context. There might be an interesting current event happening separately at the same time and you'll have a group of great guests that the audience would like to hear comment on it.
2. Prepare. A lot. You might have to interview 20, 30, perhaps even more people during the night. See if you can get a list from the PR about who is due to come and come up beforehand with three great questions for them.

"Where do you put your award?" and "What does it feel like to be nominated?" almost never produce a good answer.

3. If you can, don't go by yourself. Working a red carpet event can be incredibly chaotic and there are often lots of things going on at the same time. Having someone else there to help you cover all bases can be very helpful.

4. If you're doing a live outside broadcast and the presenter in the studio asks, "How good an indicator for the Oscars are the BAFTAs?", don't be afraid to say, "Actually, only four times in the past eight years has best film at the BAFTAs gone on to win at the Oscars."

5. Even if you're having a difficult time, act like you want to be there. What you're doing is something that only very few people in the world get to do. Most of your audience would love to be there. Even if you're cold and bored, don't talk about it. Be enthusiastic. There are lots of other jobs you could be doing instead.

6. Make sure you record an audio feed of the ceremony if you're covering an awards show for radio. You'll find a lot of good material comes out of the speeches, and it'll give you more potential news lines if you have a second machine recording the ceremony.

7. Despite the fact they're expecting the media to cover the event, you'll find that often there won't be phone reception at the venue. Talk to the publicists beforehand to ensure you have the required connections to your editors/station/ social media channels.

8. Some people don't understand why awards shows matter. I've been on the radio talking about how someone winning an award has a direct commercial impact and use data to back up that assertion. People wanted to know why and if *Moonlight* winning the Best Picture Oscar actually *mattered*. Be able to explain why it does, both culturally and in stark financial terms.

9. I often start writing a script before the show even starts. Whatever happens, you'll have a structure from which to work once it starts getting more and more busy.

10. I've said this a bunch of times but do start your report with audio from the ceremony saying "And the winner is ..." followed by the big winner of the night. It always works.

COLIN PATERSON – BBC ARTS AND ENTERTAINMENT CORRESPONDENT, RADIO 5 LIVE, RADIO 2, *BBC BREAKFAST*

What would you say to a person looking to break into your profession right now?

It is certainly a tougher and worse-paid time to be trying to break into entertainment journalism than when I started 20 years ago. However, I have loved it as a career, so do not let me put you off.

Age is massively in your favour as well. Media is now obsessed with attracting younger audiences. You have the stories to offer up which can help them work towards this.

Technology also makes it easier now to show potential bosses what you can do. Film and edit a piece for them to watch, make a radio show to which they can listen, build a website for a CV. Create your own luck.

What are the three most important things you need as an entertainment correspondent?

1. A deep knowledge. A crucial part of my job is that I can be called on to speak about a dead celebrity at little to no notice. Within 40 minutes of the news breaking that David Bowie had died, I had gone from my bed to being live on the BBC sofa. He was someone I had seen in concert, read books about, I watched his films and even conducted a self-made walking tour of his old Berlin haunts, so I could talk about him with authority. Now I am not always going to know as much about a person as I did there, but it cannot be faked. This is a knowledge built up over years, from when I was a kid. Constantly be topping up what you know by devouring interviews, reading books, watching documentaries – things you should enjoy doing anyway. This evening I just watched the Jim Jarmusch Stooges documentary Gimme Danger and found myself thinking, "I'll use some of this when Iggy Pop pops off." In the taxi on the way to the studio to talk about Bowie, I also called a friend who was a massive fan to run through the crucial points. Thanks Jon! I'm still grateful. Never be afraid to ask others for help.

2. A listener to 5 live emailed me last year and offered me very constructive feedback. He made the point that while I know my facts and figures about stars, I do not always communicate WHY people are so loved. What is it about a singer or film that connects with people? I have tried to take this on board.

3. The ability to treat stories with a degree of gravitas, despite them being entertainment. I always got annoyed over the years when people equated entertainment reporting with gossip. The entertainment industry is hugely significant to both the economy and the culture of the country. I have always believed that it is a subject which is deserving of respect. Yes, it is glamorous and there are many hugely silly aspects to it, but that does not mean that it shouldn't be analysed and reported on with intelligence. It can reflect greater trends in society – just look at #OscarsSoWhite or the troubles musicians are having with mental health.

What do you know now that you wish you'd known when you became a reporter?

I wish I had kept a much more organised contacts book. Be disciplined – store useful numbers at the end of every day.

I also wish that from day one I had started making a note of all the producers and camerapeople I've worked with. So often I am still desperately trying to remember names.

It took me a wee while to recognise that so much of the job is about being memorable. Lots of entertainment reports are very bland. If anything unusual happens, have the confidence to leave it in. Kind of annoyingly, but also kind of pleasingly, to many Radio 5 live listeners, the thing I am best known for is shouting "Bono!" a lot of times in a row at the Oscars one year live on the radio. I still maintain that I knew what I was doing, as a few Bonos in, I realised it was pretty funny. It seemed to give a lot of people a lot of enjoyment, so memorable does work.

The thing I most wish I had known before I became an entertainment reporter is that one day I would get to interview Michael Jackson on a red carpet despite being told he would not be speaking to anyone. That way I would not have asked him the single worst question of my career, "Michael Jackson, is it nice to be out and about?"

How do you see the future of your profession and what might a young person need to know moving forward?

Technology is becoming king. Keep up with it. What you can offer is an understanding of social media that your much older bosses will never have. Remember – you have all kinds of knowledge that they want to tap into.

What's the best thing about your job?

I have covered 15 Oscars, 12 BAFTAS, stood backstage at Glastonbury, interviewed many of my heroes (Woody Allen, Robert De Niro, the Cookie Monster) and been paid to watch films. I think my 13-year-old self would be pretty pleased. My 55-year-old self might be shouting at me from the future, "Grow up, it's time to get a real job."

Tell us about your favourite moment in your job?

In 2008 Jay-Z was announced as the headliner of Glastonbury. Tickets were not selling. I was at a film premiere and saw Noel Gallagher and asked him for his thoughts on this. His answer? "I'm sorry, but Jay-Z? No chance. I'm not having hip-hop at Glastonbury. It's wrong." The quotes went huge, prompting all kinds of debates about the place of rap at the festival.

A week before Glastonbury I received a call from the BBC acquisitions unit. "A Mr J. Zed's people have called asking if they can license your interview?" I obviously said yes just as quickly as if I was asked if the BBC acquisitions unit really had no idea how to correctly pronounce his name.

The following weekend I was standing in front of the Pyramid stage watching an intro film hype up the crowd by playing Noel Gallagher's comments. Jay-Z then walked on to start his set with a cover of Wonderwall. I remember standing there thinking, "This is really odd. Jay-Z is singing Wonderwall because of me." It has all been downhill since then.

(Interview with author, 2017)

5

WORKING WITH PRs

In traditional news media there is a definite antagonism towards the PR industry. It's the perennial battle of hacks versus flacks, the idea that the publicity machine is there to get in the way of journalists trying to their job, trying to uncover stories while spin doctors beaver away behind the scenes stopping it from happening. And it's true – to an extent. Managing the message, which is what people or organisations in the public eye are always trying to do, means that the idea of a reporter actually reporting thoroughly on a story in a way which might reflect badly on said organisation, or indeed merely truthfully, sets some people's teeth on edge. But the reality is, whether people like to admit it or not, the relationship between the publicity machine and the people who create content around it has always been closer than is otherwise suggested. Hard news outlets are susceptible to hype and spin and the PR game just like anyone else. You only need to look at the continued prevalence of UKIP on British television at the time of writing to see it. It's about ratings, getting eyeballs on that outlet's content, *not* telling the story – and don't be fooled by anyone telling you different.

The same is true in entertainment. Why else does everyone report on the same diet fads or movies or dress designers or cool, young artists? It's because, truthfully, 95% of the time there was a schedule or a junket or a press release alerting people to them. And even if it's not the PRs who trumpet a particular young star around all the magazines, that same wave of publicity and hype is what gets them into every single weekly rather than just one. In a social media world, where the amount of content at our fingertips is at tipping point and we need someone, *anyone*, to help us cut through the chaff, this is only going to increase. *But*, and this is an important but, the key is not to see this as a negative. A good journalist is a thoughtful one. A journalist who weighs up what they're presented with, who does their due diligence on what they see and is not so lazy as to let the PR do their work for them. It's when the latter happens that one gets the sense the publicists are running things. If journalists do their job, it won't become overwhelming.

That's because the relationship between entertainment journalists and PRs should generally be a symbiotic one, a 'you scratch my back, etc.'-style partnership to produce good, interesting content in a timely fashion. To think otherwise is facile and pointless. "The first people I met once I'd stepped through the doorway into the world of celebrity journalism, however, were not celebrities," writes author Holly Forrest in *Confessions of a Showbiz Reporter*.

> They were publicists. And it wasn't long before I realised that while the showbiz world had for many years appeared to me to run effortlessly like a well-oiled machine, it's because of these publicists who are hidden away behind the cogs spraying on the WD40. In the entertainment world, talent and originality count for surprisingly little. Publicity, on the other hand, is everything. For every unrecognised genius without a publicist raising their profile, there's a bimbo hogging the limelight with a team pushing them into the papers.
>
> *(Forrest, 2013)*

Remember too that really there are two kinds of entertainment journalism. There is the kind I'm mostly talking about here – reviews, feature content, gigs, galleries, and the like. And that does need you to get on with publicists. However, there is also a lot of investigative showbiz journalism, really good stuff in magazines as varied as *heat* and *The Hollywood Reporter*. And that is very similar to so-called hard news, digging behind the spin to discover the truth about our popular culture and its participants. If that's what you're pursuing, then, like your colleagues on the politics desk, you'll probably be putting PRs' backs up.

Initial contact

Starting to try and communicate with PR companies can seem daunting. It shouldn't be. You have to remember that their goal is to get stuff seen and noticed. They can't do their job without you. That doesn't mean you're going to get everything you want, but you do have a skill that they require.

If I was calling them cold, I always looked for the lowest person on the totem pole. A junior publicist is often assigned some of the more menial jobs in the PR office, and for them, a direct approach by a journalist is flattering. PRs are also (mostly) cool, fun people. They're enjoyable to hang out with. Suggest meeting up for a drink; schmooze a little. It'll come back to you positively in the long run, especially if they look after a nice brand. I always appreciated the freebie I got from the mate who looked after a high-end whisky company. But that's also a caveat. Don't be in it just for the freebies. PRs are under no illusion about the transaction that needs to take place between them and journalists, but it's very off-putting if you're clearly angling for free stuff. Be cool, man. These potentially mutually connections can vastly improve and increase your well of potential stories. For starters, you'll have demonstrated your desire to work benevolently together. This means you're more likely to weed out the PRs who don't care about anything but the result and instead find those "who really take the time to understand the thought patterns of journalists" (Borkowski, 2014). "Journalists, meanwhile, get deeper, richer stories from these PRs," adds Borkowski, himself a legendary publicist. "We may be living in the Now Economy, but I'd prescribe some old-fashioned relationship building."

Tell them who you are, what you're working for. It doesn't matter if it's not *The Times* or *Cosmopolitan*. Savvy PRs will realise there's a lot more mileage to be had by discussing possibilities with all journalists and that any site has the potential to have a viral story. There used to be a much more prosaic attitude – I always cringed at how parochial a lot of the film publicists were about online journalists. They were always desperate to get something in a daily paper, or a magazine that was glossy but had a declining readership, rather than a website which had millions of readers every hour every day. Some of that attitude still prevails – I guess it looks classier to have your client on the front page of a colour supplement – but it won't get more eyeballs on the product, which is ultimately the point.

You need to have a clear reason why them working with you would be beneficial. What can you bring to the table that others can't? How can you get them the most publicity with the minimum of fuss? "Be aware of the current entertainment landscape and how/where content is consumed to understand where journalism fits within," Zak Brilliant, head of distribution at movie company Icon Film Distribution and their former head of publicity, tells me. "In the digital age, access to both entertainment and journalism is forever evolving. It's smart to try and pinpoint future trends and opportunities on both sides."

Movie fan sites always had a terrible amateur rep amongst publicists, and then they realised that those places have (a) a voracious appetite for product about what they love and (b) a passionate readership with large networks, who are dedicated to spreading their love as broadly as possible. So why wouldn't you give a film's star access to a site like that? Don't feel hamstrung by the fact you're on the first rung of the journalistic ladder. Social media has levelled the playing field a lot.

Building a list

Mailing lists are vital to what I do. They're also the bane of my life. Once you start on this path, you can expect to receive 10, 20 PR emails a day. They'll say your name at the top of them, but they'll be round-robin ones. I always try and reply to a bunch of them even if it's just to say there's nothing I can do for them. Others ignore them altogether. That's fine, but you might miss something useful if you don't at least glance at every one. You can request mailing list access for things like screenings and record releases by asking PR companies. They'll probably grant you access, even if you don't actually get anything more than that. The list itself is not what's important; it's access to the things on that list. Another way to cover a lot of bases is to build a profile for yourself on a journalist services site like Gorkana (there are others). There, you can tell PRs what you're into and what kind of stuff you're looking for, and publicists will respond. Again, the contact you get will likely not be a personal service, but it's a way to increase your network, and from there you can start communicating properly with the people you get emails from. You'll also get to build your list of useful names. Be aware: you will meet a lot of benign spammers in this space too.

LUCY PREACHER – SENIOR MARKETING MANAGER, SONY PICTURES ENTERTAINMENT

What would you say to a person looking to break into entertainment journalism right now?

> Be interested in it! You have to love it and be passionate and knowledge-able about it to be a cut above everyone else. Love new types of media and technologies which will give you an edge over old school journalists. Be up for any opportunity – it's not just writing but creating and producing interesting content. And be nice to publicists!

What are the three most important things you need in terms of working with PRs?

1. Respect each other! Make friends and create meaningful relationships with your contacts. You are equally valuable to each other. No one holds the power.
2. Always appear genuinely interested in the person or brand or story that the PR has worked to get you set up – do your research and make a good impression. The PR has gone to the trouble of setting up the experience/interview, so hold up your side of the deal and be a great interviewer.
3. Do favours for each other.

What do you know now that you wish you'd known when you became a publicist?

> Working with celebrities is not as daunting as you first think. Also, I was surprised at how small my industry is. Everyone is so connected, so be nice to everyone from day one!

How do you see the future of entertainment journalism and what might a young person need to know moving forward?

> The way people consume content is different. A Facebook Live interview can potentially get way more cut-through than a front-page piece in The

Sun, so be knowledgeable about all the different outlets. Practice what you preach – make sure you are all over social media and you will have the edge.

Do you have some more tips for collaborating with publicists and getting the most out of a story/idea/junket?

Ask. Always be creative and come up with ideas and pitch to the PR. I was working on a show with Katie Hopkins, and because she is such a controversial talent, lots of publications just would not touch her. It was difficult for me to get good/favourable pieces about her and the TV show. *The Guardian* didn't want to feature her until we came up with the idea that Jon Ronson could perform the psychopath test on her. We could get a feature in the paper which was a creative angle and not promoting her, and we got a plug for the show. It also raised her profile.

Tell us about your favourite moments in your job?

Controlling the press coverage when Discovery aired the Oprah/Lance Armstrong documentary when he confessed to doping. Breaking the news of the confession, which I heard and transcribed an hour before the programme aired. I typed up a press release and circulated it. It went far and wide.

Meeting Professor Hawking – and finding out he likes to drink frozen margaritas – after a launch event for Stephen Hawking's Grand Design which was airing on Discovery Channel.

I organised a feature on *The One Show* to promote a show called *Combat Dealers*, which was about military memorabilia, and we had to park a German Sherman tank (the one from the Brad Pitt movie *Fury*) in Portland Place in the centre of London. Security weren't happy. Logistically it was a nightmare – we had to drive it down Regent Street.

(Interview with author, 2017)

How to please PRs

* *Never promise what you can't deliver.* It's very easy to get caught up in the moment and say to a publicist that you'll be able to do something you can't. There's simply no point, and it'll tarnish your reputation forever. PRs want to know what their client is getting and what they can expect from their campaigns. If you start embellishing that, explaining that if you get to come to a record launch, you can put a story in front of two million Twitter followers, when you can't, you'll end up in trouble. If nothing else, they'll ask you about your social reach beforehand and demand some kind of link to the page, so it

probably won't work anyway. That said, if you want to tell them that your student website is a 'media outlet for young people in the East Midlands' and not even mention it's part of a university, that's fine. Don't be afraid to talk up your outlet, however small, as long as you can demonstrate the figures if they ask you to.

- *Like almost everything else in journalism, you need good interpersonal skills.* "In any line of work this is valid but particularly so in a field where communications are key," says Icon's Zak Brilliant. Entertainment PRs often have to spend time with journalists – in junket hotel waiting rooms, at red carpet events, on travel jaunts to see silverback gorillas in the African jungle (seriously, this happened for a Disney DVD release). If they have a choice to spend it with someone they like and get on with rather than an adversarial pain who breaks something in his hotel room and tries to blame it on one of his peers (this also happened), causing everyone to get annoyed with him, they will.

- *Do your research.* "A well-prepared journalist is easy to spot," adds Zak. "Being informed will likely lead to better engagement all round." I've already gone on and on about the importance of this, but it's useful to see that publicists expect it too.

- *Be flexible.* "Entertainment operates across several different time zones," says Brilliant. "Being available out of hours is a necessary evil." Despite all these meticulous diaries, a lot of decision-making in entertainment happens last-minute. You need to be able to react to that without getting flustered. A lot of showbiz also happens in America too of course, either in Hollywood or New York. If British PRs are having to talk with movie parent companies somewhere in Los Angeles, then Pacific Time means you might end up doing phoners late at night or first thing in the morning. See if you can change that midnight interview, but don't whinge if you can't.

- *Circulate your coverage (so PRs know what you are writing about) and be seen out and about.* It's important that PRs put a face to the name on an email. There are some publicists that I didn't ever meet, and I never had such a good relationship with them as those I knew and hung out with. What's also crucial to a PR's job spec is generating publicity reports so they're able to demonstrate how their expertise has benefitted the client. Don't be afraid to send them links of your stuff without prompting once you've done it, or even email them something you might have done off your own back to show how invested you are in what they're trying to do. Make it look good too. If the website feature you've done on their client looks totally beautiful, for example, it will make them more inclined to come to you again in the future, knowing that you'll provide them with something that makes the product look fantastic.

- *Be first.* If you ask a PR what their favourite moments are, it's often getting someone now much more famous and successful their first big media splash. "It's particularly nice to break young talent," admits Brilliant. "Getting a journalist to buy in to a performance early on can make a big difference to someone just starting out." He remembers "getting a young actress onto the cover of a prominent Sunday newspaper supplement for her first role while she was still waiting tables in a pub". He says that "She was so embarrassed at work that day that she had to go home. Her mum bought 50 copies of the paper for everyone in her home village."

In other words, don't be afraid to take a punt and get in on someone before they're a big name. They may be anonymous now, but they might not be in a year's time.

Protecting your integrity

A lot of this comes down to your ethics. It's very easy to get sucked into the world of so-called 'churnalism', where PRs are able to take advantage of time-poor journalists and essentially use them as an extension of the machine pushing the brand narrative, failing to see them as an entity which works within the system but is necessarily sceptical about it as well (Borkowski, 2008). But the simple reality is that entertainment journalism generally works according to diaries and significant events and is about access. This is mostly controlled by public relations companies. As I've suggested elsewhere, *Empire* wouldn't consider itself part of churnalism, but its journalists do write about the things that they get access to, and they are not going to criticise that or do anything to break that relationship. They would argue that they give bad reviews, but what they really do is take what the PRs give them and then expand and deepen that context. They rely on the patronage of publicists, but then utilise their journalism skills and nous to create content that entertains and informs their audience beyond mere puffery. The same is true elsewhere.

But if you ever feel yourself compromised, don't fret. Every professional journalist has been in that situation, and most of them haven't made the ethically correct decision. The system isn't perfect and neither are you.

Going directly to the famous people

One of the great innovations of social media is that it has made celebrities more accessible. So you might feel like you want to avoid publicists altogether and approach famous people straight off the bat.

Sometimes it can work, depending on the level of celebrity. You might also have interviewed a star in a more traditional manner and had such a good rapport that you can then speak to them more directly in the future. I've found my greatest success with going straight to stars is when I've done "Where are they now?"-style features and the person in question is not quite so famous. I tend to use the pro version of the Internet Movie Database (IMDBPro) which often lists cinematic people's direct contact details. The Screen Actors Guild in the US used to have an invaluable service where you could phone them up and they'd provide you with three actor contacts at a time for free (sadly, this service no longer exists unless you are a recognised casting agent, and I've yet to be able to get round this). Smaller actors and bands and artists and designers might also be gettable, and there's this amazing thing called the phone book, which some people are actually still in! But while it's worth checking out this more direct route, it's only likely to be successful very occasionally. Cynics would point to this as being evidence that public relations has taken over the world. They may be right, but it doesn't mean it has to damage your journalistic endeavour.

Being an influencer

"Storytelling is still the industry watchword," writes Mark Borkowski on *The Drum* (Borkowski, 2016). "But the way it is understood varies massively. To look, for example, at the entries for this year's Cannes Lions is to see the blurred lines between the PR function and digital marketing and content creation."

Icon's Zak Brilliant echoes this point. "The traditional PR flack/journo relationship is certainly changing," he says. "When it comes to feature films, studios are becoming more and more risk-averse and less likely to work with press. Why take a risk on something you cannot control?" He explains this is why "more and more focus on social media "influencers" who can generate awareness to a target demographic through positive editorial, all paid for." His advice is that "Anyone starting out today needs to be aware of these shifts and understand how to navigate around them. Certainly a good understanding of social media is absolutely fundamental."

Money – and the sheer amount of it spent on the biggest parts of showbiz – does mean that clients are more careful. But as Brilliant suggests, this also means there's incredible opportunities to approach what was traditionally a very arcane system in new and exciting ways. You may not work for Buzzfeed, but as discussed above, can you open up innovative methods for a PR's client to spread their message without compromising what Mark Borkowski dubs the "brand narrative"? As a young journalist, it's important that you don't think traditionally – yes, there are well-worn systems in place, but they're ripe for disruption by the right people in the right way. This has, in effect, been happening for some time with celebrities, for instance, choosing to talk about politics on a cult podcast rather than appearing in a straight magazine profile piece. If you can take that philosophy of telling a brand (or person's) narrative in a different manner, or position your outlet as a way for someone or something to be presented in a unique and beneficial way, you'll be a valuable asset to publicists – and the PR machine. And you'll still be able to do good work, I promise.

Ten top tips – working with PRs

1. PRs are people too, honest.
2. Remember all their names; keep a proper contact database. I didn't and it cost me.
3. Be prepared to do them favours. If you cover something small or seemingly insignificant that they're promoting, it'll most likely pay off down the road.

4. Publicists are contacts just like anyone else, and you are one of theirs. Check in with them periodically to maintain the relationship.
5. Just like journalists, PRs love to socialise. Buying them a couple of drinks here and there can pay huge dividends.
6. PR can be a good way into journalism. An internship with a marketing company doesn't mean you're stuck there forever, and it can give you more understanding of how the system works.
7. You don't have to be working for a big outlet to get PRs on your side and access to talent/stories. They have to provide reports for their client of any press coverage, and while they'd prefer a big feature in *Elle* or *The Guardian*, a blog post is still publicity. This is particularly true for things like restaurant relaunches, which don't tend to get covered by the mainstream press.
8. If you get PRs on your side and start getting invited to launches and the like, you can swap forking out at the supermarket for free canapés.
9. Start small. If you're just starting out, you will probably not get access to Coldplay or George Clooney. You may however be able to review a small art movie or talk to Sky Living's latest reality star.
10. Don't mess PRs around. They can be frustrating occasionally; for instance with non-disclosure agreements, or embargoes. And you shouldn't be in thrall to them by any means. But if you try and buck the system too violently, you'll be black-balled, which isn't a good look when you're at the beginning of your career.

CHRIS SMITH – CELEBRITY EDITOR, MTV UK

What would you say to a person looking to break into your area of the profession right now?

> Know your stuff and don't act like you're above it. An encyclopaedic knowledge of reality shows/celebrities isn't something to be sniffed at if you're planning a career in showbiz journalism. You may have aspirations that surpass writing about reality stars, but in order to get there, you've got to do the hard graft first, which may or may not include creating an article about a Z-lister taking out the bins.
>
> Also be sure to clean up your social media – make sure it represents you in the best possible light. If you aren't engaging in the conversation about the people/subjects you want to write about, why would employers think you're a good fit for the job?

What are the three most important things you need as a multimedia news and features showbiz journalist?

1. The ability to spin a story with a unique angle – everyone is covering the same thing in the world of online journalism, so you need to be able to grab the attention of your reader and stick out in a sea of copycat articles.

2. Understand that visual aids are just as important as words. Even the most hilarious, engaging, pithy piece about Kim Kardashian will likely flop if you're promoting it alongside a dull/generic picture attached to your social media post. The same goes for the content of the piece. People's attention spans are short; use all the tools at your disposal to keep them on your page.
3. When interviewing a celebrity, always remember you are there for a story, not to become their best friend. You are first and foremost a journalist, not a presenter. Obviously you don't want to be rude, but if you've got seven minutes with, say, Reese Witherspoon, don't waste four of them trying to win her over, because that's four minutes of wasted time.

What do you know now that you wish you'd known when you started out?

That social skills and well-placed confidence are just as important as being able to create good content. Whether you're interviewing a huge star, trying to get a quote at a swanky party or just working with a PR to secure time with talent, if you can't read how to handle the person you're talking to, it's not going to work. You could go in all guns blazing, piss them off and leave with absolutely nothing.

How do you see the future of your area of the profession and what might a young person need to know moving forward?

To be a great multimedia journalist you need to be multiskilled and willing to learn. You don't just need to know how to write. You need to know social media like the back of your hand – it is such a central part of digital journalism. You need to know how to video edit, be able to use Photoshop and even have basic animation skills – Snapchat changed the game with how younger people consume their news. If you have the skills to write, produce, edit and design, you're head and shoulders above your contemporaries.

What's the best thing about your job?

Meeting incredible people and going to unbelievable places. This job can and will take you anywhere if you persevere and work hard. I've been lucky enough to go to the Cannes film festival numerous times, fly to various locations for junkets and interviews (I once got flown out to the Maldives for a week to chat to Joss Stone for 20 minutes), and interview huge stars such as Brad Pitt, Emily Blunt and, of course, S Club 7.

(Interview with author, 2017)

6

USING SOCIAL MEDIA

There will be many who think this book should actually have been called *Social Media ... and Entertainment Journalism*, such is the central nature of social media within the life of a modern showbiz hack (indeed pretty much every hack). But while I'm relegating the practice of social media to a single chapter, I can't overestimate enough how fundamental your utilisation of social networks will be to both your success in this job and your day-to-day experience of doing it. While social media has been one of the biggest tech disruptions of all time, it's also provided a great many avenues for aspiring journalists. Many of my colleagues who started as more archetypal 'writers' and 'editors' now have 'social media' as part of their job title. Social media companies are branching out into content, which is beneficial to a new journalist. The great thing for you is you don't have to learn as much. Anyone coming of age now doesn't remember a time before Facebook, Twitter, Snapchat and Co. It's part of your DNA. It's something you do in your personal life without thinking. But that's not to say you should pat yourselves on the back and think you've got social skills all wrapped up. Checking and maintaining your personal Facebook feed is not the same as approaching it from a professional perspective. Blurting stuff out on Twitter and randomly following people is not the way you handle it if you want to use the site most effectively. And the process of 'social-ing' your content and distributing it profitably requires certain best practices. There are other excellent books dedicated to the general function of social media (though the problem with them is that they have immediate built-in obsolescence every day that they exist and social media evolves). What I cover in this chapter is a broader insight into how an entertainment journalist might use social media and some specific tools you can engage immediately as regards your attitude and what you create to ensure you have a higher chance of success.

Facebook versus everything else

The ethical questions about whether Facebook itself should be classified as a media company are for another place, but there's no doubt that right now it's the most important social media space in the world for journalistic content. And it knows it. The Facebook algorithm, the mathematical formula which dictates how content is positioned on the feeds of over two billion users, is something that's talked about in hushed tones in journalism offices around the globe – if you can crack it, the thought is, you've essentially won the Internet. So yes, Facebook is king, with Instagram, Twitter and Snapchat coming up behind. And that's why live video has increased so dramatically over the past year, with Facebook focusing on it and launching their Facebook Live video apparatus. Periscope and Meerkat may have laid the foundations, but Mark Zuckerberg's crew has since grabbed that market by the scruff of the neck and now dominates. Remember too that money talks here. Boosting your posts on Facebook by paying to promote them can dramatically affect how successful they become. The good news is that at the moment it's currently not punitively expensive if that's something you want to do. That might well change moving forward.

The jury is still out as to how much Twitter actually benefits audience figures. It's a crucial part of an outlet's media strategy and visibility, but lags behind Facebook in terms of its conversion to actual page views and loyal audiences. At the time of writing, despite teams already having been assembled to concentrate specifically on creating and disseminating material through its platform, Snapchat is still a comparatively youthful participant in the game. Its impact remains to be seen – there's no point in me shouting out a bunch of figures here that could change completely by the time this book's published and again in three months from then. The picture-based Instagram has expanded beyond selfies with Instagram Stories and Instagram Direct, but as of now, it tends to be used more as a marketing tool than a direct journalistic one. It's phenomenally popular of course, particularly amongst celebrities and those who pursue the goal of celebrity (hence the rise in so-called Insta-models/stars/whatever). It's also, inevitably, owned by Facebook, bought for $1 billion in 2012. As for YouTube, I would contend that it's a media platform rather than a social media one – though I'm sure there are enormous arguments to be had there.

A jobs market

This is all about the conversation. Social media – specifically Twitter and Linkedin – is a place where you can appeal to and talk directly with editors and influencers who are in positions to offer you work. One freelance colleague started writing for an online outlet after she engaged in Twitter discussions about feminism with the deputy editor of said workplace. Internships and "Come work with us" or "Anybody know a good …" requests for talent are fired out by people all the time. There are weekly virtual 'meetings' in which anyone following a certain hashtag can participate.

Following the feeds of people you like or want to impress is also a great way of understanding them. The features editor of such-and-such keeps tweeting about hedgehogs? Pitch them some kind of showbizzy hedgehog story. The host of your favourite podcast always links to music videos by barbershop quartets? Time to woo them for an internship by @-ing them into interesting videos of close harmony singing. I remember hearing stories of an extremely powerful television executive who commissioned shows based on very random and not very televisual hobbies he had. Knowledge, as they say, is power.

There is also another slightly dubious trend of people getting hired according to how many Twitter or Instagram followers they have, or how many likes on Facebook. Remove the suggestion that it's possible to buy online fans (never do this!) and this is one way to raise your currency in the job market. Cultivate a following; follow lots of other people; engage in the community; share funny or interesting things that reflect your professional world view. Think about your ideal platform too. Hopefully, you'll have a solid presence on most of them, probably focusing on one more than the others, but as discussed in Chapter 8 on multimedia, it's important to consider what works for which platform. Are you trying to show off your wit? Twitter's good for that. For longer writing, maybe Facebook? Instagram or Snapchat tend to be more visually focused (although images are vital on all platforms). There is no magic bullet for having a massive social fan base as a media bod – other than being famous for something else as well or doing good stuff well and hoping for the best; but not only does it demonstrate that you understand the capacity and impact of social media channels, it also shows employers you're happy to envelop yourself in the world. Everyone likes the idea of having an influencer on their team.

Finding stuff

A few years ago, a Hollywood-based paparazzo had a very lucrative career following a bunch of young Australian actors on Twitter and then showing up at the places they said they were eating/partying so he could get their picture. Because they were new to town, but already established stars down under, he had minimal competition and was able to flog the photos to the Australian celebrity magazine market. One can still do that – and of course people do – but you have to be a bit cannier if you want to grab an exclusive. There's also the dark side of this practice. Between 2008 and 2009 a group of young Angelenos burgled a series of homes belonging to high-profile stars when they were out. How did they know? They checked their whereabouts on social media.

Still, the direct line you have to celebrities and their daily lives via social media means that you have a broader scope for thinking about interesting questions to ask people, or potential ideas to pitch that might tie in with a pop cultural trend you find on Instagram. If nothing else, there are just a shedload more famous or almost-famous people to write about. Do you follow the next Justin Bieber on YouTube? What's trending? There's also useful tools like #journorequest, a hashtag to help you find a contributor or maybe some information you haven't been able to dig up. Embracing the community side of social media is vital. It can feel very isolating sometimes, and the negativity that it breeds often makes it appear like an inhospitable place. But if you come at it with vigour and precision, there is much to be found out there.

It has also become a repository for the lazy journalist to turn a quick story around. User-generated content has been rebranded as social content now, but social media is a quick way to gather vox pops or filter opinions about a hot story of the day. In lieu of getting someone on the phone, ripping celebrity tweets or Facebook posts or Instagram pictures with their captions have become stories by themselves. If one's being honest, this can be useful. The media environment doesn't pause these days, and if you're asked by your boss to turn a story round quickly, access to high-profile 'quotes' are valuable. On the other hand, there's a fear that this trivialises journalism, that it reduces the role of the journalist to a mere aggregator, that it perpetuates the view that the entertainment media is constantly cannibalising itself. As with most things, it's a little from column A and a little from column B. As a journalist it's *always* worth searching out that extra original something. But if you're in a bind, then social media has provided a relatively simple get-out.

NIKKI CAIN – DIGITAL STRATEGY EXPERT, PERCOLATE

What makes a story sing on social media?

There's two types of 'sing on social' when it comes to content. Firstly, and most simply, is clickbait. This is the sort of Shareable.net content you see on Facebook, that has a picture of a gorilla with a kitten and the tag line "Gorilla saves a kitten, but what happens next is just unbelievable." The same would apply for news; for example, "You'll never guess what Beyoncé has named her baby."

Clickbait is exactly what it says on the tin; it's content made to make you click, but not necessarily share well. In other words, this is about return on investment (ROI) for link clicks and not about building and maintaining a loyal and engaged audience. So while it may look like content is receiving a large volume of traffic from social, it's not engaged or loyal traffic and the bounce rate is likely to be high. It also won't perform well on social algorithms, which are designed to favour shared content and keep clickbait at bay.

Secondly, viral or influencer content. This is content that shares well or is awe-inspiring or aspirational to its readership. Viral content is the 'golden ticket' for news websites, usually resulting in huge traffic surges, link backs and a boost in algorithm timeline slots and SEO search results. Platforms like Buzzfeed look to obtain most of their traffic from viral content. In terms of what makes it 'sing', it's about producing a powerful emotional response with something simple, whether that be shock, awe, happiness, compassion – if it causes a reaction, it'll get shared. There can be exceptions to this, most of which relies on how people wish to be perceived on social. For example, celebrity news may be read by more individuals than it is shared by, simply because a large percentage of social media users are not the type of persona to be proud of the fact they're reading celebrity news. Users of social are very protective and thoughtful about what they share, thus anything that makes them look funny, clever or 'ahead of the curve' is more likely to be shared.

To what extent should a person think about social when creating 'non-social' (i.e. broadcast or traditional print) content?

All non-social content would still have a talking point, which should have a social presence – as this is where talking points tend to end up. It wouldn't be relevant if it didn't have a social presence already.

Is it possible to make something go viral?

There are certainly companies that will claim they can do this but, in essence, not truly. The very meaning of the word 'viral' means it takes off on its own accord and is an unstoppable force. There are certain pieces of content that are most likely to go viral, but it's usually something organically cultivated. However, there are certain people and companies who devote their time to finding viral content across the likes of Reddit and Tumblr and have such an influence on social that most of their posts will do very well.

What are your top tips for a young journalist to effectively use social media?

1. Be present – engage in debate, follow everything, pay attention to news topics.
2. Burst your bubble – social media is one big echo chamber – the people you follow tend to be the people you agree with most – but branching out of that is so important to gauge reality and find content you wouldn't necessarily find otherwise.
3. Use resources wisely – spend time learning how free tools like Buzzsumo work, use Feedly and spend time on Reddit and Tumblr to source content.
4. Think psychology – social is ALL about psychology. Get into the mindset of your followers and understand what makes them respond, what they like and don't like. Most importantly, understand what social media is used for – a lot of it is about pride, boredom and validation.
5. Be careful what you say – social has a footprint and it doesn't go away when you delete it. Everything you put online, expect to be accessible forever.

6. Rule of thumb – if you question it, don't do it. If you make a mistake, apologise quickly and accept responsibility; ignoring it will make it a story. Never be the story!

What do journalists get wrong when they approach social media?

If you're not going to do it properly, don't bother at all. People who join platforms and don't follow the platforms' 'social norms' will stick out like a sore thumb and alienate themselves. If you don't have time, don't bother.

Social should be at the forefront of all journalists' minds; it's an indicator of interest and a starter of fires. Playing down its importance is content suicide. While the news has always set the agenda, the agenda is cultivated, mutated and moved on by social.

Does a journalist need to be good with all social, and if so, why?

In short, yes. The essence of journalism is communication and social platforms are full of just that. While it may be a new skill to learn and an ever-evolving one, the story is always where the people are.

(Interview with author, 2017)

What makes a great entertainment social media story?

- *An intriguing sell.* The Internet is a cluttered place, so there's a reason why you have such teasing headlines on social media. It's an invitation you can't turn down, an opportunity to be part of a club, a chance to see someone you thought you never would. Obviously, you need to be careful these don't turn into clickbait. In other words, don't promise something you can't deliver. Don't over-egg the pudding. And be aware that when a user clicks through a social link, they want to feel like there's something to engage with. That's why "Guess what so-and-so looks like now?" headlines are hit-and-miss. Yes, you'll probably get a click-through, but once you've seen the picture, what else is there? That potentially raises your bounce rate (the rate by which people ditch your story within a few seconds), and engagement rather than page views have become a much more reliable barometer of success in today's marketplace.
- *Emotion.* Does the story stir something inside you? A lot of successful Facebook posts are about amazing things that make you feel great. It may be a strange feeling for a journalist, but joy and positivity, as opposed to cynicism, actually work very well on social.
- *Digitally native.* Is it something that was born online? Like a Facebook Live video? Obviously, social companies trumpet stuff that utilises and promotes their own tools, which is why so many media outlets have embraced

Facebook Live. But the phrase 'digitally native content' is an important one. Is it something that was specifically targeted at Facebook users, or was it just a story that you happened to create and that you've shoved onto social platforms? This is where research comes in – what is trending on Instagram today? What are the topics of discussion on Twitter right now? How can you insert something you create into that conversation?

- *SEO (search engine optimisation).* Yes, it stands for search engine optimisation, but the typical definition of what SEO entails has become a bit archaic recently. Keywords still matter and so do headlines. Fresh content being frequently added to your page will elevate your SEO profile. This is all true. But where a socially savvy journalist can exploit Google's SEO (and while there are other search engines available, let's be honest and admit Google is the only one that matters whether you like it or not) is by tapping into common searches to finesse their content. One editor told me that he goes to the question-and-answer site Quora and looks at the entertainment-themed questions for feature ideas. Reddit is a good source of material too, especially for entertainment content. Another method is getting 'advice' from Google's autofill function. When I typed in "Which Star Wars …" on the address bar today, suggestions for what I searched included "Which Star Wars character are you?" "Which Star Wars movie is the best?" and "Which Star Wars movie should I watch first?" None of them are spectacularly original ideas, but there are three possible features you could write that you know would play well with SEO as they are commonly searched for Star Wars queries. Doing the same thing with "How Marvel …" suggested "How Marvel movies are connected".

- *Going viral.* It's hard to make this happen. A virus is something that just arrives and takes hold rather than something you actively try to attain and know when it's going to hit. So don't focus on trying to create something viral. Instead, create something shareable. If it's shareable and enough people share it, that's when it goes viral. If you put the cart before the horse, you're likely to fail.

- *So what makes it shareable? Generally the topic is fairly mainstream.* Niche doesn't tend to work in big, broad strokes, as you can imagine. The image attached to the post should help you lure in the audience. Funny is always good. In the early days of email, jokes were endlessly forwarded between friends and offices. So if your content makes people laugh, you're doing well. The concept should be simple – is the story or idea you're selling easy for an audience to grasp? Can it be done with the sound turned off? It's why you should always aim to have subtitles for any video you make for social – most people look at them at work or while they're doing something else, so they almost always won't have the volume turned up initially. And of course, you've got to make it mobile app-friendly.

- *Research your social media audience.* They might have slightly different tastes to your audience as a whole. Look at the comments on outlets' Facebook pages, their other social feeds – see what discussions and debates are being had and shared there.

- *Gamification.* Think of ways that you can engage your audience in interesting ways. There's a reason why quizzes are such a prevalent part of Buzzfeed's front page – they know how shareable it is to find out which member of the *Friends* cast you are most like or how much you know about David Bowie cover versions. For your audience, a lot of social media (as witnessed by the fact you have to 'like' something to acknowledge it) is about showing off to your friends, knowing something before someone else, showing yourself to be part of the important conversations. It's the 21st-century equivalent of the water cooler. If social-ing your content is about marketing it and creating social referrals (people clicking through to your main brand/outlet), then you've got to be endlessly surprising and innovative. This might involve live-blogging something, posting your interviews as live video, giving people a two-element multiple-choice question and getting them to retweet or favourite a tweet depending on which reply they choose. The great thing is there's room for experimentation here, which helps young journalists because employers and outlets are looking for answers that are almost impossible to guess or predict, even for those with experience.
- *A lot of it is luck.* You can follow all the rules, consider all the above points and create something you're convinced will appeal to a social audience and it'll go nowhere. Alternatively, you'll knock something off and it'll become a sensation. There are definite trends for what makes a viral story, but remember a lot of it is down to computer software. Facebook's algorithm is constantly being tinkered with (especially in this post-truth media environment), and it's a secret as guarded as the original recipe for Coca-Cola. Do everything you can to make things go in your favour … then cross your fingers and hope.

Verification

Truth is always central to a journalist, but in a world of bots, anonymous accounts and fake news, there's a potential for this to be harder than ever to attain. Craig Silverman, in a 2012 issue of *Nieman Reports*, disagrees, saying, "Never has it been so easy to expose an error, check a fact, crowdsource and bring technology to bear in service of verification." (Silverman, 2012) This is true, though of course distrust in the media is at an all-time high and presenting the objective truth doesn't necessarily mean that people will still believe you.

But in this fast-paced world with deadlines impending and editors breathing down your shoulder, fact-checking – particularly in the entertainment world – can be something that's ignored. After all, it's only movies, or music; they're only celebrities, not politicians; this isn't a terrorist attack so why should it matter if it is 100% accurate? Well, it should. And if you're going to utilise social media to find and craft and source interviews for stories, you better be sure that you're doing your utmost to verify everything. Social media is littered with instances of wrong information based on rumour and innuendo. It's important that if you are going to report something that's unverified, you at least label it as such (though making sure you're abiding by the law). Knight and Cook write in *Social Media for Journalists* that "there is no such thing as an anonymous source, only sources whose identities are not revealed to the public" (Knight and Cook, 2013). It's important that if you do use material gleaned from a pseudonymous social media account, *you* know who it is you're talking to, even if the audience only know their nom de plume. The Internet and social media have broadened the scope of stories and people you have access to, but that also means it's more difficult to confirm who they are.

Knight and Cook argue there are five rules to abide by – "develop your instincts … crowds are wise … admit when you are wrong … be cynical … [and] know the landscape". These are all good skills to have. Admitting an error in particular is vital. As they write, "Sometimes a story can be so powerful, so explosive, so tempting that the thought that it might not be true is dismissed; these are the stories that can damage a news organisation irreparably." (Knight and Cook, 2013) They can do the same to your reputation.

As Silverman writes,

> Spreading facts requires the use of narrative, powerful images and visualization, and appeals to emotion. We must engage readers in ways that help them get past their biases. It also requires that we dedicate ourselves to spreading the skills of verification and fact checking within journalism – and to the public as a whole.
>
> *(Silverman, 2012)*

And finally … engaging the trolls

In a word, don't. I've been told by a reader that he hoped I died, just for writing a jokey piece about *Indiana Jones and the Kingdom of the Crystal Skull*.

Giving oxygen to people angling for a fight is not worth it. People are very passionate about their pop culture heroes. If they love a movie you don't or think you've been too harsh or too biased about a band they adore, it's unlikely that engaging them in a factual debate will result in a nuanced discussion. After all, so much of entertainment is subjective. We find this comedian funny and this one not; that record is the greatest one of the year; you wish that singer would hang up his guitar and get a different job. If you like the joust, then by all means go for it. My guess is it'll be about 14 tweets before they call you a fascist.

Ten top tips – utilising social media effectively

1. Facebook is more important than Twitter.
2. For the rest of time, there will be media outlets trying to second-guess the Facebook algorithm. If you can do it, you'll have a job for life.
3. Several journalists I know have now moved on to jobs more focused on social media. So learning about it can increase your career prospects.
4. A good Facebook headline is about 70 characters long.

5. Scour social media regularly. It can help you come up with the story ideas that outlets will be commissioning in the future.
6. The 'sell' you write for your piece when you put it on social will probably be the most important thing you do with the story.
7. Consider how you're going to sell a piece on social media before you pitch it, and finesse accordingly.
8. Think about how you might utilise socially native video, like Facebook Live, in your stories.
9. You might want to think about promoting or 'boosting' some social media posts. It doesn't have to be *that* expensive and will put you in good standing with the networks.
10. Presenter-led video doesn't work so well on social. Most people watch it illicitly and can't have the sound up. You can use subtitles, but format-wise, it doesn't feel so effective.

JULIA WHITE COHEN – MEDIA PARTNERSHIPS MANAGER, TWITTER UK

What makes a story sing on social media?

> Shareability. This is something different to 'clickability'. You might click on a link about Kim Kardashian, but you probably wouldn't share it because you might not want to admit that she's your guilty pleasure. But something that is emotive, informative or relatable will garner many more shares, as it acts as social currency for the sharer. Think about what it takes for someone to click the share button and put their name to that content. For the same reason newness performs well, being the person who broke the story to their community first always has value.

To what extent should a person think about social when creating 'non-social' content?

> All content has the potential to be social – even if it doesn't obviously feel 'social'. Always think about how you will promote, present and play out any piece of content in the social sphere. You might even want to create spin-off content just for social. For example a long-form video interview might get cut into subtitled sound bites for Twitter or Facebook. Or you might do a live Snapchat Story behind the scenes at a movie premiere to promote your review. All of this drums up eyeballs for the central piece of content.

Is it possible to make something go viral?

> Often the content that goes most viral comes from an unexpected source and is not necessarily created by the media or a content brand. A good

example was 'the dress' that sent the Internet bonkers – all from a debate between friends on a personal Tumblr account. However, you can certainly predict the types of content that are likely to be shared most on different social platforms and create content appropriately.

What are your five top tips for a young journalist to effectively use social media?

1. Be social – have a presence on as many social networks as possible so that you keep up to date with functionality changes, algorithm tweaks and how different content performs on each platform. Running your own social channels isn't that different to running a newspaper's or a magazine's channels – lots of the skills transfer – so the bigger and more engaged your following, the better it will look for your CV.
2. Mine for stories – social media is an absolute gold mine of story fodder. Story potentials lie all over social networks and there simply aren't enough paid journalists to cover them all. So keep your eyes peeled, know how to spot a good story, and don't be afraid to reach out to people, sources and potential contributors via social media. People expect it these days – and it's a brilliant way to crowdsource.
3. Find your voice – the voice is the single most important attribute to getting social right. Find a niche subject area and a strong voice and share/ participate in interesting discussions and you will gain a strong following. Don't be formal and don't hold back – be bold.
4. The conversation – an easy way to get noticed and create strong content is to follow the conversation and add value. Keep yourself up to date with what's trending, and if you can, wade into the conversation with something of use. Trending topics across the social networks are the ones with the biggest eyeballs.
5. Work your network – if you're job hunting, make the most of the opportunity of open platforms like Twitter to reach out to potential bosses. Say something smart or add something of use to a conversation and you will get yourself noticed. Be honest too – don't be afraid to ask someone for a job. I got my job at Twitter by contacts I had nurtured on the platform.

What do journalists get wrong when they approach social media?

I think journalists and brands who get social media wrong underestimate how intelligent their audiences are and try to force too corporate or formal a tone. Social (whatever publication you are writing for) is about having a voice that reflects the values of the journalism but also speaks to people on a personal level. Those are the accounts people will want in their everyday life – and in their newsfeeds. The accounts which people can't live without.

Does a journalist need to be good with all social, and if so, why?

It's something you just can't avoid. Even if you don't feel you want to post personally, set up professional accounts and play around with what works and what doesn't. Most jobs these days will require some element of social media – you can't expect it to be left to the 'social team' anymore. So showing knowledge of what works and what doesn't work on social media will be a vital string to your bow. From keeping on top of the latest news to sourcing and following up stories to posting your own stories – social media is really at the heart of the journalistic process right now.

(Interview with author, 2017)

7

REVIEWING

There are lots of young writers who want to be reviewers. There are, I believe, lots of reasons for this, and most of them aren't good. The misconception that it's easy, that it involves little other than espousing your opinion, which you are convinced that everyone wants to hear. The fact that you get to go to gigs and movies and get records and meals for free (okay, this is definitely one of the perks).

Reviewing – at least reviewing something really well – is difficult. It requires precision and context. Our 24-hour media culture demands that you must turn reviews around quickly and under circumstances not conducive to reflective thought (one music critic I know has to write his while sitting in the station waiting for his train back to the country straight after the concert around midnight). It's appallingly paid. Mostly gone are the days of journalists like Pauline Kael and Lester Bangs, who wrote sprawling critical essays that were pored over by huge audiences (though it's worth checking out the *New Yorker*'s Pulitzer Prize-winning television critic Emily Nussbaum if you're interested in that sort of thing, as well of course as Kael's and Bangs' own books). When seminal film critic Kael wrote her review of *The Sound of Music* for *McCall's Magazine*, it was a big deal. Ditto her piece about Orson Welles, called "Raising Kane". When a modern-day reviewer writes something controversial, it will go viral for a short while – *The Times*' film critic Camilla Long seems to be pretty good at that – but is soon forgotten.

Yet, when I talk to journalism students, the articles they always pitch to me are reviews of this or that performance or place. Simple, they think; straightforward …

Well not really. For one, they're not going to be one of a small crop of people reviewing that particular product. Social media and the Internet age has meant that mass reviewing is now the norm. And it's been boiled down to its essence – a thumbs up or down on Netflix, a user rating on the Internet Movie Database, a star system. In other words, you have to be doing something *really good*, or really different, I suppose, to stand out from the crowd. Some critics fear and are frustrated by the encroachment on their so-called territory. The BBC and *Observer* critic Mark Kermode isn't one of them. "There's a misconception about the internet, which is that blogging is changing and devaluing criticism," he told the *New Statesman*'s Bim Adewunmi in 2013.

> It hasn't. At the beginning of any new way of dispersing information, there's a kind of sense of anarchic freedom: you suddenly have a gaggle of voices. When Roger Ebert started doing his TV show with [Gene] Siskel, people wrote essays about how it was the end of criticism. What they didn't realise is that it's just another way of doing it. ... It will settle down and the good will emerge and it will come down to the same basic rules: are you doing the job properly? Do you know what you're talking about? Are you contextualising? Are you writing wittily and entertainingly and engagingly?
>
> *(Kermode, cited in Adewunmi, 2013)*

How I write a review

First, stop and think. Actually thinking about the thing you're going to review is, like listening in interviews, one of the most obvious parts of the processes yet the one most people forget to do. There is a large part of reviewing which is about accessing the gut – how do you *feel* about what you've just seen or heard? But while the urge to follow that more instinctive emotion blindly is strong, it's also just one aspect of the craft. Consider what you've just witnessed. When you've experienced something so viscerally, with the goal of making a judgement about it, it takes a while for those thoughts to coalesce into a shareable opinion; at least it should for a professional reviewer. Talking about amateur film bloggers, former *Daily Mail* film critic Chris Tookey says, "A vehement statement of opinion is held to be enough. It isn't – or rather, it shouldn't be."

I started off taking notes when I reviewed movies but gave up, partly because I felt like it didn't really help me and partly because I couldn't read what I'd written when I left the cinema. But when you're starting out, it might be worth forcing yourself to do this, ensuring that you jot down a random thought in the moment that you'll be able to crystallise into something more well crafted and concrete later on. Or you might simply jettison it – I remember writing notes about plot points in movies and why such-and-such hadn't been introduced or talked about or explored yet, only for it to happen one scene later.

While it's sometimes difficult to expand on any aspect of the review due to space, it's crucial that you still try to avoid making generalisations. This is really the problem with star ratings – is one three-star movie the same as another three-star movie? How much worse is a one-star play than a four-star play? Putting a star rating at the end of a review may be expeditious, but, says producer Rebecca O'Brien, "it demeans and diminishes criticism" (in Falk, 2011). You might not have a choice. The outlet you work for might utilise stars or thumbs or some variant on that, but the underlying learning point remains in terms of how you frame your review as a whole. "It's a shame you're effectively reducing things to just a thumbs-up or thumbs-down," movie producer Duncan Clark told *Moviescope* magazine, "especially when there's so much material that kind of slips into a greyer area than that" (in Falk, 2011).

I'm also, believe it or not, thinking about my integrity. My teeth still go slightly on edge when I remember a film magazine asking me to up my one-star review to a two-starrer because the film's leads were in the same edition of the publication. The 'honour' of critics is constantly under attack, especially in the social media era. A music journalist friend says the most common – and in his view baffling – comment he gets under most of his gig reviews is "Were you even *at* the same gig as me?" His response – which he's long since given up on doing – was, "Er, yes, can't you tell by the way I describe it, even if I've got a different opinion about it to you?" Film criticism, which is what I used to practice, even had its own major scandal when in 2000 Sony Pictures used quotes from a fictitious movie reviewer called David Manning, who they'd created to puff their product. The non-existent Manning apparently worked for *The Ridgefield Press*, which is based in Connecticut, USA, and 'he' gave great reviews to films like *A Knight's Tale* starring Heath Ledger and a (terrible) comedy called *The Animal*. *Newsweek* uncovered this hoax as well as the fact that Sony had got employees to talk in TV adverts about how good Mel Gibson's *The Patriot* was, rather than using real cinemagoers. It got so bad that in 2005 the distributor settled a class action lawsuit which asked for refunds on tickets bought to see the films Manning had praised. Sony was asked to pay out £850,000, and the legal agreement stated that anyone who'd bought a ticket to the films which Manning had lauded between 3 August 2000 and 31 October 2001 could demand £2.80 for their ticket. Obviously, this is an absurd example, but it speaks to the fact that audiences are both bound by and sceptical of reviews. It's one of the first things you turn to when you're looking to invest in a product, yet chatter about, say, TripAdvisor is often that people who had a negative experience are much more likely to post a review than those who had a positive one, because they're angry about what they've experienced and feel the need to vent. But in terms of *my* integrity, I want to make sure that whatever I write or say about what I'm reviewing, I don't feel compromised by making that opinion public and I would be happy to back it up further if asked about it in more detail. Former *Mail* critic Chris Tookey got so fed up that he created a website (movie-film-review.com) which calls out reviewers who seem to regularly crop up on posters for films, lauding even the most spurious of quality. Trust me, you don't want to get a reputation as a 'quote whore'.

Ultimately, though, I'm trying to be truthful. Being truthful is harder than you think when you write. Most of the content you create is filtered through some kind of prism. That might be the outlet you write for, the mood you're in at the time (many films either suffer or benefit from this, as recognised in the Sundance Effect, where average movies are inappropriately lauded because of the high altitude and intense festival vibe) or whether the reviewer is trying to achieve something specific at the time (like wanting to fill the review with gags to show off their humour). When I write a review, having thought long and hard about what I'm reviewing, I try to empty my mind of everything and consider what's being reviewed in very simple terms (this will be explored further in the next section). I try not to think about the bon mots at first, about the sly turns of phrase – I'm not a person who can do that instantaneously, although there are some better writers whose prose is naturally thus – and instead focus on the nitty-gritty of what I'm trying to convey. The flourishes come later.

If I can be authentic when I review, if I can remove myself from the phony surroundings of a screening room at 10.30 a.m. on a Monday morning and instead place my mind in a throbbing multiplex on a Saturday night (if I'm doing something mainstream, for instance), then I can write something truly fair and honest. "Always tell the truth," writes Barry Norman in his book *And Why Not? Memoirs of a Film Lover.*

> If you think the film is crap you must say so, no matter how much you may hurt or offend the people who made it. Your obligation is not to them but to the viewers who might, on your recommendation, spend a small fortune taking their families to a cinema. If you're going to tell these people that a film is worth the financial outlay you'd better be sure you mean it.
>
> *(Norman, 2002)*

As to what actually goes into it? O.D.C.A.E. Or C.O.D.E.A. Or whatever anagram you want to make out of Mark Kermode's excellent five parts of a great review, which in his case relates to film, but could be applied to anything. In his book *The Good, the Bad and the Multiplex*, Kermode boils down a great review to five ingredients: O for Opinion; D for Description; C for Contextualisation; A for Analysis; and E for Entertainment. This is pretty much spot on. By the end of the review you should be in no doubt as to what the reviewer thinks of the thing he or she has reviewed. You should have a precis of the plot or, say, what it depicts if it's a painting. You should know about the historical framework within which it sits; for example, how many albums the band has made previously or whether it's the first all-black production of *A Midsummer Night's Dream*. And it should be funny and intelligent and informative and engaging all at the same time (Kermode, 2011). This sounds like a lot. And if you want to, you can expound on it over 5000 words, if you're offered the opportunity. But I used to write 80-word DVD reviews for *Empire* for £10 a time, and I attempted to do all of this in each of those too. I'm sure I failed most of the time, but I tried – and you should too. Film critic Barry Norman, who became famous for his BBC show in which he critiqued the week's releases, was more pithy, saying that he concocted an imaginary viewer who was impatient and brighter than him. His goal as host of the show was simple – to explain to this person, without being boring, who was in the film, what it was about and whether it was any good (Norman, 2002).

QUENTIN FALK – FREELANCE FILM CRITIC, FORMERLY OF THE *SUNDAY MIRROR* AND THE *DAILY TELEGRAPH*

What would you say to a person looking to break into film reviewing right now?

> Think twice – but don't be deflected if you are passionate enough about writing reviews even if there's no money in it ... at first. And keep the 'day job'. The various film-related magazines are always looking for cheap labour, but you'll need to be thick-skinned as you will get more rejections than acceptances – even if you think you're the new Mark Kermode or Wendy Ide. Check out IMDB and you'll see a proliferation of film blogs on the review site, some elegant, many less so. Start your own blog as that might be a possible way in.

What are the three most important things you need as a film critic?

1. I've always specified three elements in writing reviews: inform, illuminate and, if possible, also entertain. Those are, of course, generalisations.
2. The ability to try and place your review in some sort of context. Every film, high or low budget – and, arguably, both – should be treated similarly if there's a paying public involved at the exhibition stage.
3. Passion is a requisite and knowledge of film. Not necessarily in a nerdy sense but in such a way that your review will carry more gravitas because of your understanding of the medium and its participants.

What do you know now that you wish you'd known when you became a movie critic?

> When I started writing reviews it was simply a case of Cinema versus TV, with the big screen fighting for survival against the force and intrusion of the small. Then video entered the equation before the eventual explosion of multiplatform.
> I never remotely envisaged this kind of future for creative moving imagery when I first entered the fray firmly on the side of the big screen, and my words were/might have been, on occasion, predicated on the background of that early conflict.

How do you see the future of your profession and what might a young person need to know moving forward?

> When I talk to students about reviewing, I now tend to emphasise the diminishing power, if that's the right word, of the traditional reviewing

clique. I say, perhaps a little simplistically, "You are now the most powerful critics thanks to the proliferation of social media."

It's no coincidence that when a movie is being previewed to a general audience, the presiding executive/PR will often tell the audience: "Don't forget to tweet your reaction." 'Word of mouth' – a phrase once used glibly by producers/distributors possibly to try and counter the effect of poor print reviews – is in some quarters now regarded as the be-all and end-all for a film's box office prospects despite the millions poured into publicity and marketing.

What's the best thing about being a film critic?

If, as in my case, films are/were my passion, how rewarding to be able to write about them, sharing whenever possible my enthusiasm, see them for free, and get paid for the privilege.

What are some of your favourite moments from your career as a film critic?

In 1969, I'd just started writing my weekly film column for the *Wokingham, Bracknell & Ascot Times* – on which I was an indentured trainee – when I had a letter from a reader following my review of *Midnight Cowboy*. She wrote (to the editor): "You used not to have a film critic. You now employ the bizarrely named Quentin Falk. His remarks concerning *Midnight Cowboy* suggest the former situation should be returned to as soon as possible." Happily my editor didn't accede to her request although admitted in print that I was indeed "bizarrely named".

In 1987, having become a freelance critic, I returned to *Screen International*, the trade paper, having five years earlier finished a four-year stint as editor before leaving for the *Daily Mail*. One of my first reviews – on *Screen* you were required to assess not just the film but also its box office prospects – was for *Cry Freedom*, and I was a little lukewarm in my appraisal. The result was a furious response from the distributor, which then banned me for a few weeks from its press shows as a reprisal.

Don't ever weaken in the face of reader or, in this case, industry pressures. Always write it as you see it.

(Interview with author, 2017 – and, full disclosure, the author's father)

Five other things you need to know if you're going to review stuff

1. *People won't always listen to you – and that's kind of annoying.* The very nature of reviewing is it's about ego. You think that your opinion is more valid than other people's and it's important to share it. That imbues a reviewer with quite a bit of power. Any author who has experienced a dip in their number

of stars out of five on Amazon because someone gave the book one star (often because the delivery was late or wrong) will know that. Yet if you establish an audience of some kind or work somewhere high profile, it can be comparatively easy to think that what you say should go. In some ways, that's the kind of person you need to be as a reviewer, although not as aggressively idiot-like. So imagine one's shock when you say something's bad and everyone ignores you and buys/sees it anyway? Welcome to the lot of a reviewer, especially in a time when mainstream entertainment is a lot less nuanced than it used to be thanks to the fragmentation of the marketplace and the amounts of money involved in creating product. "I think most movies are critic-proof which is, I suppose, a very depressing thing for me to admit," writer and broadcaster Jason Solomons told *Moviescope* (Falk, 2011). The important thing if your opinion isn't being taken seriously is not to change it or second-guess what you think people want to hear. Don't just say something because that's what everyone else is saying. When I vote for the BAFTA film awards, I always feel like my choices are completely different to what the majority of the membership are putting on their ballots (and it's generally played out by who ends up getting the prizes), because I don't care what everyone else is talking about, only what I like. But you know that people vote for things because they want to say they voted for the winner or because they couldn't be bothered to watch everything and were subject to confirmation bias about what's got buzz.

You also, of course, might have got it wrong. "I walked out of [David Lynch's surreal 1986 classic] *Blue Velvet* when I saw it," Mark Kermode told the *New Statesman*. "I stormed out and wrote a really angry review of it. Three years later I went back and saw it again and realised it was one of the greatest movies ever made." According to Kermode, "Part of getting it wrong was part of the learning process." He explains, "What I discovered from *Blue Velvet* was, if a movie really gets under your skin, you can go either way with it. And whereas it's possible to love great movies and hate really bad movies, it's the movies you love and hate at the same time that are really exceptional." (Cited in Adewunmi, 2013) So there!

2. *70 per cent of what you review will be average to crap.* "In my view about 70 per cent of films, like 70 per cent of everything else – plays, TV, books, music, whatever – range from the tolerable down to the execrable," writes film journalist Barry Norman. "Of the other 30 per cent most are good, some are very good and one or two are nuggets of pure gold." His advice is that, "If you are a professional critic the best you can do is accept the odds, reconcile yourself to the fact that disappointment probably awaits you but always approach the next film with optimism. Without that optimism, you're in the wrong job." (Norman, 2002)

In my early days of reviewing for *Empire* magazine, or the now defunct *Flicks*, I watched some really bad and really boring films. I still don't understand what was going on in *Twilight of the Ice Nymphs*, and I dare anyone to watch Rhys Ifans in *Twin Town* without wanting to smash up the cinema in rage at how rubbish it is. But there are a lot of great moments – when you walk into a cinema knowing little to nothing about a movie and see something truly transformative, which you then get to talk about to everyone who'll listen; or you hear a revolutionary piece of music that does something new with the form; or you watch a play that defies categorisation and manages to be hilarious, bleak and provocative all at the same time. You've got to want to talk about those things, but be aware that you'll also spend a lot of your time trying to make a three-star review sound fresh and interesting, unlike the material which necessitated it. Writing raves and writing bombs are much easier than writing about something that's a bit 'meh'. If you're going to practise, I would do so by creating a bunch of three-star reviews – it'll hone your craft much more effectively than penning a takedown of *Transformers* number whatever.

3.   *Respect your audience.* I'll leave this one to esteemed American film critic Stanley Kauffmann. "I discovered early the special pleasures and benefits of writing regularly for a group of demanding readers," he wrote in 1966. "The continuity generates a relationship both with them and with one's critical self, past and future, that cannot be reached through occasional criticism." He goes on, "I cannot imagine a more stimulating life for a critic of new works than to be able to address regularly a group of the best readers he can conceive of and to be given a free hand in doing it." (Kauffmann, 1966)

4.   *Recognise, or at least acknowledge, your bias.* We all like particular bands or a certain film-maker and are often willing to defend him, her or them when those around us are not. It happens to the greats – Pauline Kael was often accused of being soft on director Brian De Palma. I've argued how important it is to be truthful, but sometimes that truth is unconsciously corrupted. As a critic, this can be hard to spot as most of it is happening without us realising. But as long as you are honest with your audience – and remain honest with yourself – you'll be okay.

5.   *Find your own way to do it.* There are so many ways to disseminate your information now. One of my students has just launched a YouTube music review channel as she's frustrated at the lack of female critical voices within the music industry. Some are doing it in tweets or via their Facebook feed. There are, of course, still review pages in newspapers and magazines and online. But what's so great about a disrupted journalistic marketplace is that it provides you the opportunity to try and do something new. There are only a few people who have genuinely altered the form. Pauline Kael was probably one of them, so successful was she that she inspired a group of acolytes known as the Paulettes. Iconic US critic Roger Ebert pioneered the thumbs up/thumbs down format with his colleague Gene Siskel on their TV pro-gramme. Nick Kent helped change the way music criticism was done back in the 1970s, and Charlie Brooker was ahead of his time as a TV reviewer in *The Guardian*. This is but a small sample, and things continue to be in flux. So abide by the so-called rules and ethos of criticism that hopefully you can glean from this chapter, but also consider how you might take it forward. The

first recorded film review was published on 15 June 1896 (the film was *May Irwin Kiss* and the critic didn't like it) – times have changed since then, and how we engage with reviews and critics should too.

Ten top tips – reviewing

1. I learned how to write reviews by basically copying the ones I read in *Empire* when I was at school and inserting the actors/films that I was watching into the body of the text. Don't plagiarise of course, but it's a useful way to practice and see what works when you're getting started.
2. House style is crucial. How does the outlet you're writing for do things? Do they use a star system or emojis to determine how good a movie is? Do you have to write the artist and venue at the top of your review, or do you need to include a brief synopsis of what happens? What kind of language do they use – can you swear, or should you use industry speak?
3. I'd avoid using first person in reviews when you start out. It seems counter-intuitive, since a review is the definition of your own opinion, but unless you're a well-known reviewer hired specifically for your point of view – Mark Kermode, Camilla Long, Jay Rayner, etc. – it can seem a bit self-indulgent. Most of the time, at least as a young journalist, you're writing as the voice of the outlet you work for, rather than strictly as yourself, so it's worth trying to avoid first person.
4. Writing a bad review is easy; so is writing a rave. Writing a review about something average is where the real craft comes in.
5. If you're writing a bad review, it can be easy to let yourself go overboard and be more cruel than you need to be simply because you have a great simile you want to unfurl. Don't be that person.
6. Remember the context of the thing you're reviewing. No one sets out to make anything intentionally bad, so try and consider that when you're writing about it. There might have been a tummy bug going round the kitchen that night, or there might have been budgetary issues on the movie you've just seen. That doesn't mean you have to write your review particularly differently; it's just worth remembering there are people and hard work involved.
7. Be prepared to stand by your review, but at the same time don't be afraid to admit you were wrong subsequently.
8. Often circumstances mean you have to turn reviews around quickly. But it's always better to sit with your review for a while if possible so that you've had time to clarify your opinion and ensure it's not simply an emotional reaction. That said, sometimes you're specifically asked to provide an immediate emotional reaction, which is fine.
9. Don't go with the herd, but don't be deliberately contrary because you think it makes you look cool. Be honest.
10. People are more likely to accept your bad reviews if they know that you are equally voluble when you talk about something you love. Charlie Brooker

made his name thanks to his eviscerating and hilarious reviews of TV programmes he hated or found ridiculous in *The Guardian*. But they only worked because when he watched something he loved, he was evangelical about it. An audience gets tired of endless antipathy and negativity.

DAVE SMYTH, CHIEF ROCK AND POP CRITIC, *EVENING STANDARD*

What would you say to a person looking to break into your profession right now?

It's an exciting, transitional time. There is doom-mongering across the journalism industry at the moment, of course, as veterans find that the way they are used to doing things no longer pays the bills.

But on the Internet there are more outlets than ever before, and the field is wide open for people with fresh ideas to take things in a new direction entirely. Also, younger journalists can be more valuable in a period when the technology side of things is changing so rapidly, simply because they tend to have a more natural understanding of this stuff than the generation above them.

Hopefully someone out there can finally crack the way to make it start paying well!

What are the three most important things you need as a music journalist?

1. Depth of knowledge. Everyone's a music fan. You need to be the person who really understands it, who gets the way it all fits together. That means reading books, not just Wikipedia, and listening to things outside of your comfort zone. Devour everything.
2. The ability to do exactly what you've been asked. I'm amazed at how many professional journalists, when asked for 1000 words by Tuesday lunchtime, will provide 1300 words by Thursday evening. You don't need to be the greatest writer of all time – if you're reliable and make life easy for your editor, they'll keep commissioning you.
3. Better ideas than the others. There's no point coming to an editor with "I want to interview Coldplay." They'll have already thought of that and will have better access than any freelancer. Come up with the really interesting stories, angles or trends that they might not have thought of before.

What do you know now that you wish you'd known when you became a music critic?

That, as with all journalism, it's basically just about people. As a younger writer I think I was much more of a music snob who would turn his nose up at writing anything if the music itself wasn't spectacular. Now I realise that an interesting, charismatic person or band with a great backstory will make for a far more entertaining article.

How do you see the future of your profession and what might a young person need to know moving forward?

I think it's less possible to do it as a pure writer now – if you can take good photos, make great playlists, talk confidently into a camera, design a slick website and write as entertainingly in a 280-character tweet as in a 2000-word feature, you'll be a much more valuable journalist.

What's the best thing about your job?

Getting to see some incredible concerts that I know I would never have got tickets for as a normal punter. Getting to pick the brains of some of my heroes. Travelling to some wonderful places for interviews.

I've ended up feeling more a part of the music industry than the journalism industry because I work from home so in person I see more of musicians, music publicists and record company people than I do my actual boss – and music people are 99% really cool and lovely. And now I'm a bit older, being a freelancer who manages his own schedule has also been great in terms of being able to spend a lot of time with my wife and children.

Tell us about your favourite moments in your job?

There have been a few mad experiences. Ozzy Osbourne grabbed my hand, thrust it under his shirt and made me feel the metal plate that he'd had inserted after his quad-biking accident. I was taken on a private jet to an Ibiza hilltop to hear the second James Blunt album. Prince tweeted a link to my interview with Lianne La Havas, which is probably the closest I'll ever get to being knighted. I was allowed to sit in deadmau5's Ferrari for upwards of 12 seconds. And if I correctly understand the lyrics to a single from grime rapper Stormzy, he mentioned in song the fact that I interviewed him in the *Evening Standard*.

For a most memorable moment, I'll go for Ásgeir, who brought me out to Reykjavik, then drove me in his own car for hours through the sparse Icelandic countryside to visit his childhood home in the absolute back of beyond. I had lunch at the farm of his guitarist's parents, met the sheep, then coffee and cake with his parents another few dozen miles into the wilderness. There was also a tiny gig in the remote church he used to sing in as a child. To spend that amount of time with someone and gain that much insight into their life, in these days of half an hour in a hotel room, was really special.

(Interview with author, 2017)

8

WORKING WITH DIFFERENT MEDIA

All through this book you'll find professionals vociferously advocating a broadening of your skills. They're correct – understanding how to code and edit video and manage social channels can and probably will be vital to having a successful career over the next 50 years. However, I'd add a caveat to that. You want to be a journalist, not a cameraperson. You want to be a journalist, not a web developer. Understanding those abilities and having a grasp on them is great, but always remember that you're looking at them and using them through a journalist's eye. In other words, this book isn't a technical guide to using a JVC camera. Or a user's manual for an Edirol voice recorder. But what this chapter should do hopefully is alert you to the sorts of things you should be considering and aware of as an entertainment journalist working in today's multimedia, multiplatform environment.

NB: I'll also add that the central thesis of this book assumes that a modern journalist is one whose material appears online in some form, so I'm not including 'working on the Web' as a form of multimedia.

Video

Video, to paraphrase *Zoolander*, is so hot right now. Its use online has risen over the past decade as consumer cameras and their accompanying codecs improved and broadband got better. Nowadays, it's being prioritised by a lot of media companies mainly due to the fact that selling ads against it makes more money than standard online adverts. Those adverts before the video starts on YouTube or Yahoo? They're called pre-rolls, and they are a lucrative money-spinner for the content creators. We've also talked elsewhere about how the concept of engagement has become more valuable to outlets than simple page views. Videos tend to generate longer engagement times from an audience. Finally – and crucially – Facebook and

Snapchat have become video evangelists, especially with socially native video spotlighting it on their platforms.

Shooting yourself

As budgets have been squeezed, you'll often be tasked with shooting a premiere or perhaps an interview without a professional cameraperson. It will be down to you, a journalist, to produce material of a professional standard that will go onto You-Tube, Vimeo or your native platform. So you've got to be good enough to measure up to a person who might have a number of years' experience and be paid specifically to shoot something. As such, I again asked Ben Robinson, a former entertainment cameraman turned moviemaker and film productions guru at the Doha Institute, for his best advice if you're handed a camera bag and told to go and get some great footage on the red carpet.

- *You need to know your camera and lens and the whole set-up of your kit.* How many memory cards you have, how to format and back them up and deliver them safely to the content provider. How long your batteries last and when to charge them. "Very important is back focus on certain cameras," says Ben, "where the picture can become very blurry and unusable if the back focus is not regularly checked and maintained". He explains that "differences in temperature can also affect this and can also affect white and black balance, which both need to be checked regularly." He says, "Lots of camera ops forget to adjust black balance, which can lead to strange picture aberrations." And "Likewise, if your white balance is not adjusted for each location, you can end up with overly blue, green or orange pictures – depending on the clash with the white-balance setting the camera is currently on." A simple tip here is to turn on the 'full auto' setting on your camera. Manual settings will mean you have more control over each individual element such as exposure or white balance, but it always means mistakes are easily made if you're not familiar with the kit. Most semi-professional and above grade cameras shoot solid, HD, TV-ready footage now (and that includes your smartphone). If you have it on automatic, then you'll be able to think about the other creative aspects of what you're shooting, like questions and B roll.
- *The other thing that can get you in trouble is bad audio recording.* "When I see a camera op not using headphones to monitor their audio, I know they're an amateur," says Ben. "If the boom mic or radio mic is not set up properly, you can get very distorted, unusable audio, which will destroy the shoot." If you're shooting on something like a DSLR camera, then make sure you have a good enough microphone and audio set-up to capture the audio the way you want to. Just leaving the mic sitting on the top of the camera and then hoping you'll get professional level sound at a raucous event like a premiere or launch is idiotic. A video piece won't work unless it's got quality sound to go with it.

Explains Ben, "You need to make sure – especially with news and fast turnaround packages – that you are delivering to the producer and editor a package that is technically solid," adding that you must check "the memory card contains enough good shots to build interesting and eye-catching sequences that have enough variety to allow the producer/editor to tell the story they want to tell and know that they have all the shots they need". He says, "I have been told that I helped at least five up-and-coming reporters/presenters boost their career because my footage/coverage/visual flair made them look dynamic and allowed them to tell the story they wanted to tell. Don't just tiredly churn out coverage of an event with no imagination." Ben notes that, "Obviously, if it's a press conference, your options are fairly limited, but generally I used to treat my assignments like mini movies. Beyond the basic required coverage, I always tried to provide eye-catching establishing shots, a couple of artistic cutaways and good lighting on interviews."

- *Don't shoot random, unrelated footage that will never be used and just clogs up hard drives.* Shoot with the story in mind – discuss at length in the car on the way to the shoot to ascertain what the producer wants. Avoid conflict with the producer – you may think you know better, but remember we are shooting for their package. "Do excellent work and don't argue, be graceful under pressure and offer positive creative solutions and you will build a reputation," says Ben. And talking of memory cards, always back them up and guard them with your life. It's easier than ever now to catalogue and back up material as you go, in the cloud. Don't get asked for the key interview at the end of the day only to find that you've either wiped it or dropped the only copy somewhere between the location and the coffee shop where you bought your lunch.
- *Get a trolley!* "I would say 85% of camera ops have back problems," admits Ben. "Ignore the mockery and get a strong trolley with bungee cords and large and strong enough wheels that it won't topple. My trolley became my best friend on long shoots." His advice is, "Travel light on shoots, but not incomplete – over time you will master your kit bag and lighting kit."

A number of my students have walked into the equipment loan shop in their first term and found their calling. They love learning about and handling the cameras and spend the majority of their course trying to get better at it. So let's say you want to do this camera thing more regularly? I asked Ben for some extra guidance. "I would recommend finding a mentor, an experienced shooter who is willing to take you under their wing and teach you the basics and tricks of the trade," he says. "This stuff takes three to five years to become a master, but there are many shortcuts you can learn to deliver excellent packages within months" (some of which you've just heard about above). For those of us who watched with envy as the print journalists wandered round the Cannes film festival in shorts holding a notepad and pencil while we lugged two boxes of lights, a tripod and a camera down the Croisette, sweating and swearing as we went, the concept of physical fitness is a given in the cameraperson trade, even if it's not a profession you would immediately associate with needing to be in shape. "You will get a bad back if you're not physically fit and training on core muscle strength," says Ben. "It's almost guaranteed (ask me in five years' time from now if you ignored this)." He advises, "Go to the gym, do Pilates, do stretching, wear the right clothes and shoes. Look after your health – it is manual labour essentially (albeit with complex technical skills involved)." You should also, he adds, "be competitive and invest in training and equipment where possible".

What's also great about working in video is that you're at the coalface of new and emerging technologies. VR, 360-degree – these are all techniques that are evolving and being applied to journalistic video. "There will always be a future for this profession," Ben argues. "The technology is changing rapidly so you need to stay on top of these updates on a daily basis. The platforms for this content seem to be shifting – traditional TV will always be there, but online platforms and traditional TV are in flux." He adds, "I wouldn't want to define that myself – but you need to be studying the field constantly. If you learn to be a great, innovative visual storyteller that can align themselves closely with the story being reported on, you will be a great asset to any organisation."

Ultimately, being a good cameraperson can be brilliant for a number of different reasons. "If you're into technology, you get to inhabit a very technologically complex world and hopefully master it," says Ben. "You also work long hours with your colleagues. These friendships have stayed solid long after the job ended." Ben goes on, "And if that's not enough, I hung out with Jean-Claude Van Damme on a yacht in Cannes – he was in a particularly wild and humorous mood. Plus another time, we stopped someone committing suicide by being in the right place at the right time!"

TV

One of my first jobs was working on a daily entertainment show for Channel 5, and this was the place where I found my journalistic feet in terms of interviewing, editorial and leadership skills and a sense of story. I can still remember randomly putting my hand up when someone asked if anyone wanted to interview the cast of *Cold Feet*, not really sure if it was okay to do so, and then being sent off with a cameraman and a big dollop of hope to see if I could get something decent. Entertainment shows like those – *Exclusive!* and *The Movie Chart Show* – exist to a much lesser extent now in the UK. In the US, there are still plenty of syndicated showbiz magazine shows like *Entertainment Tonight* and *Access Hollywood*, but it's a dying art form in Britain. Instead, that kind of subject matter has migrated to the online pages of newspapers and magazines as well as nestling – unfortunately some might say – in the folds of mainstream news programmes. You might also see them somewhere in the never-ending labyrinth of cable, on MTV, etc. and on shows like *BBC Breakfast* and *Good Morning Britain*. So forging your path in traditional entertainment TV journalism has become more difficult, but that's not to say television doesn't need showbiz hacks, whether it's reporting and producing on red carpet events for a breakfast show, co-ordinating content on *Film 20*-whatever or booking and preparing celebrity interviews for *The Graham Norton Show*. There's also, dare I say, a space to explore longer-form entertainment content on documentary strands like *Dispatches* and *Panorama*, though in a more investigative way. Certainly, with a former reality star currently in the White House, the conduct of the mainstream media under public scrutiny and stars playing activists on social media, there's never been a moment where popular culture has intersected with so-called hard news as it does right now.

So if you are wanting to work in telly, what do you need to know? Well, it tends to pay better than print journalism. Working in TV was my most lucrative period, but that's because generally you are on a short-term contract and you're freelance, so the job security isn't so good. That's compensated for with a fatter pay cheque. That freelance nature means that often the hours are peculiar. If you're working on a particular show, then you might be cramming a few weeks of work into a few days as it approaches broadcast, and often programmes need to be turned around fast. I spent a few months wandering around the Sky compound in south-west London ('Skyberia', as it used to be known by its inhabitants) in the middle of the night while working as an entertainment producer on a morning show. Having lunch at three in the morning gets tiresome very quickly.

The development team at an independent production company can be a good place to get a foothold in the industry. There is a lot of writing involved (such as pitches to commissioners) and it's creative. But depending on your success, it can be gruelling, and it's likely companies want to refresh the pool of people generating ideas every so often. Still, as an insight into how the industry works and in terms of progressing to different areas within the business, it's always a good place to start.

Above all, you need to be a visual thinker. So many people who try to make video 'stuff' think they can take an idea that would work better in print or on the radio and just stick some pictures over the top of it. That's what qualifies as a good piece of video? No – it sounds obvious, but you have to be thinking about how something would look. My first question to any student who pitches a video idea to me is "Okay, but what do we see on screen?" Often, the answer isn't forthcoming, or it's "I'll just put B roll over the top of it." That's not good enough. Your mentality has to begin with the moving image on the screen. What would make for an arresting, visceral experience as a viewer? How is the audience going to interact with what they see?

VICTORIA HOLLINGSWORTH – FREELANCE TV PRODUCER/ DIRECTOR

What would you say to a person looking to break into TV right now?

As there are so many different production companies and so many different genres of television programme, first I would advise that they decide what area of TV they are interested in by watching as much as possible. If they are, for example, really interested in reality TV programmes, then make a point of watching them and getting to know the formats, or if it's game shows, then have a think about some ideas for games that would work. Secondly, make a note of the production company/companies who make the type of programme you are interested in – this is always the last thing that comes up on screen when the end credits roll. Then you know who you need to write to with a CV and cover letter. Do your own research, Google the company, see what else they make and look at who the key staff are. You want to be writing to the head of production or anyone they list as being in charge of hiring. See if they run any programmes for work experience or if they have runner jobs, and make your cover letter as targeted as possible. Don't be afraid to use flattery! Especially if they make your favourite programme.

What are the three most important things you need as a TV professional?

1. I think a crucial quality you need to be a TV professional is to be a self-starter. When I am hiring a researcher or a runner, I want someone who can use their own initiative.
2. Bring ideas to the table. TV is often about problem-solving and teamwork, and having someone on the team who can help come up with solutions and ideas to help develop the programme will go a long way.
3. Being a good negotiator. TV can sometimes be more about crisis manage-ment, especially when you are dealing with budget constraints, difficult con-tributors, balancing different personalities on the production team and managing expectations of the commissioning editor. You need to be able to handle the huge variety of unpredictable situations that you will find yourself in and be able to think clearly how to find a solution without losing your head.

What do you know now that you wish you'd known when you became a TV professional?

Be confident – in your own abilities to do certain things and take on challenges and also confident that work will come along. It can sometimes be tricky working as a freelancer and never knowing where your next job is going to be. Also keep a record of your contacts. Sometimes I have filmed with people and not kept a record of their contact details and then been frustrated when I've needed to get in touch with them again.

How do you see the future of your area of the profession and what might a young person need to know moving forward?

I think moving forward it is vital that people entering the profession are as equipped as they can be to ensure longevity in their career, and this means being versatile. More and more programmes are 'self-shot' by the director with little contribution from a professional cameraman. So you need to make sure you are competent with a camera and understand the basics of how to film a sequence and how to frame an interview. And keep your notes on all this too for you may find you don't need to do it for years and then suddenly you are asked to go out and film, and you want to be confident enough to take that on.

What's the best thing about your job?

By far the best thing is the variety. It is an utter privilege to work on different programmes that allow me to immerse myself in a subject I may, at first, know little about and spend time speaking to world experts, asking the questions that the public would want answered. It has allowed me access to some very special places too, and I feel very grateful to have had the opportunities I have had.

Tell me about your favourite moment/s in your job?

I think for pure pleasure and fun, the best moments were when I was presenting *A Place in the Sun*; we would often film in the most stunning places and witness breathtaking sunsets and vistas. It is also where I met my husband (he was my cameraman) so I shall always treasure that time. Working as a producer for Sky One's *Showbiz Weekly* was also a great job. I loved the travel, especially my time filming at the Cannes film festival each year. Always utterly exhausting but we found time to have a lot of fun too!

(Interview with author, 2017)

Audio

When I was growing up in the mid-1990s, listening to the radio was mostly about hearing the latest music that I liked and occasionally an interview with a band on BBC Radio 1's new-music show in the evening. Entertainment content has always existed on radio – one could argue that the entire output of most stations is entertainment content – but showbiz within the parameters that I've laid out in this book is in rude health. Whether it's entertainment bulletins on Radio 1 or celebrity interviews on commercial networks like Magic or Absolute, radio gives audiences a chance to spend a little longer with someone, and a good interview – something like *Desert Island Discs* on BBC Radio 4, for example – is an opportunity to hear a whole different side to a famous person. As such, from an entertainment journalist's perspective, there is a lot to engage with on the air. You could be a more traditional news producer, or you could be a broadcast journalist working on a particular programme, booking and researching guests. Further, you could – as colleagues have done – make radio documentaries. Music-themed ones, as you can imagine, work incredibly well.

There is often a perception that audio is 'easier' than video. That's patently false, of course. Doing anything well is always going to require skill and hard work. Yes, it sometimes might be easier to make people relax in front of a mic as opposed to sticking a camera in their face, but there are often other challenges in radio. For example, you might be interviewing someone live who's in a completely different location to you, sitting in a booth somewhere, while you try and make it feel like a cosy chat in the studio together. If you decide you want to speak on radio too, there are a host of skills you need to be good at. One is being in control of your voice. Excellent presenters are able to sound engaging and conversational without making the sound levels shoot all over the place. There's a performative aspect to it to, just like any presenting job. A friend who occasionally steps in as a guest presenter on a major national station says that it's one of the hardest things he's ever done. Not only do you have to be aware of what's going on in the studio at that particular moment, but you're also thinking about the impending news bulletin, keeping your eye on anything breaking, checking when the weather and the traffic are happening, or making sure you are not talking into the ad break. Not only that, but you're thinking about the four guests you've got on during your three hours; you've already prepared questions, you've read their books, listened to their new albums, been to see their films. And you might have to leap from a serious news item about a gun attack to the weather and then straight onto a live two-way interview with a Hollywood star. It's hard. Exhilarating, absolutely; a magic trick of luck and skill and adrenaline. But still very difficult. It's not, repeat not, just sitting in front of a microphone and chatting.

But what radio gives you that other mediums don't is that sense of intimacy, a camaraderie as you sit with your headphones on the train or in your car. Done well, it's an experience like no other, and as a journalist, that provides much opportunity.

Podcasts

Perhaps the greatest innovation in audio over the past few years, though, has been the rise of podcasts, a term that came about as a shortening of iPod and broadcast. Podcasts have afforded media outlets and individuals the opportunity to speak with their audience in more depth and in a much more direct way about their brand or a topic.

What podcasts do is that they provide you a chance to create something you're passionate about in a personal way and utilising comparatively cheap technologies. Yes, you can get yourself a soundboard and expensive microphones, but it's not necessary. As long as you have decent sound (some podcasts are recorded directly onto a computer), most podcasts can get away with it, although thinking about the professionalism of your output's audio is something you should definitely take into consideration. But the two most important things you need for a good podcast are really high-quality content and excellent marketing. Are you doing something innovative? Or are you at least bringing something new to the table? There are now hundreds of real-life crime podcasts thanks to the success of *Serial*, but they will only have the chance to break through if the listener feels that what they're getting is something they can't find elsewhere. Will it be an interview podcast or a zoo-style chat podcast? Are you going to have sections that you do each week? What's the frequency? Original content is crucial, so the answer to the latter question should be weekly or fortnightly at the very minimum. If you've built up an audience already, then you might want to produce a TV-style season of episodes like the Hollywood history podcast *You Must Remember This*. Do your research about what's already out there and don't just waffle on. Optimum length for a podcast at the beginning is probably between 20 and 30 minutes. Any longer and, while you might please your loyal audience, you'll find it difficult to attract fresh listeners who feel daunted by having to download an hour of something they're not sure about.

Regarding marketing, podcaster Imrie Morgan, who co-hosts the show *Melanin Millennials*, in a conference appearance at Coventry University in May 2017, pointed out three vital elements in the making a successful series.

- *The artwork is fundamental.* Does it tell your audience what the show is trying to do and say? Is it striking and eye-catching? Does it look professional and thought-through, letting the audience feel like they can trust you to provide them with an engaging and enjoyable listening experience?
- *Think about your network.* Like a lot of online media, podcasts can benefit vastly from being promoted on social media by other more successful podcasters. Think about creating a link with podcasts that might give you impetus (though be wary about approaching someone who's doing something incredibly similar to you and asking them to say how great you are). Research your niche and embed yourself in the community so that those within it might feel inclined to trumpet you to their friends.
- *Don't go into podcasting expecting to make money.* The monetisation around podcasts is still nebulous. This doesn't matter so much if it's the audio offshoot of an established outlet as the likelihood there is that the ultimate goal is to drag more people towards that brand in general. But if you're doing it for yourself, don't underestimate your worth and be prepared for the finances to start slowly. (You might want to investigate a crowdfunding platform like Patreon, which is definitely an avenue for podcast producers.)

It's not a guarantee of success, but if you come up with a great idea and execute it engagingly and informatively with charismatic on-air characters and good-quality audio (before marketing the hell out of it), it's a good start.

Editing

I'm a decent editor using Adobe Creative Suite (Premiere Pro for video, Audition for audio), but might still just be able to remember Final Cut Pro 7 and the open-source program Audacity. While many media courses try to convince you otherwise, there is not an industry standard editing tool. Lots use Adobe, lots use the Avid system, etc., etc.. Once you ensconce yourself in the software itself, you'll find that the visual grammar of them all is pretty similar. While there are different hot keys and protocols for each, it's a bit like learning Italian if you can speak Spanish and/or French. Not totally unfamiliar, though still requiring a great deal of practice. Most programs allow you some kind of free trial – I suggest downloading that and giving them a whirl. You'll most likely find the one you're comfortable with. To extend the language metaphor even further, editing skills require practice. Lots of it. There's no way round it – you just need to sit and play with it for a bunch of hours and work out how to do it. You can teach it to yourself (and the endless online tutorials are generally pretty good and will help you if you get in a bind), but it's about graft. You haven't truly been an editor until you've sat up until three in the morning fiddling with a series of tiny little cuts until they're as perfect as you're able to make them.

As I say, though, I'm not a professional. I'm a journalist who can edit and, as such, herewith some guidelines to making it work effectively for you.

- *Log your shots* – transcription is always one of the most boring things you'll do as a journalist, listening back to the interview you've just done and writing out what was said. It's also the most important. Re-familiarising yourself with the story you're telling, thinking about what was said and how it was presented. There's a temptation not to log all your shots – going through your footage and jotting down time codes and notes (if you're super lucky, you might have an intern who does this for you, but it's increasingly rare) – but it's more than worth it. When you're deep into the editing process and you need a particular shot, or a specific quote, it'll be easier to dig it up if you know the point at which you captured it during the shoot. Logging your material also helps to solidify how you might tell the story visually in your mind.
- *Paper edit* – sometimes called an assembly edit, this is a rough cutting together of your material. You don't need to use finesse here; it's more about creating a basic shape. It's also likely where your script will start to be written as you'll know at this stage where you need explanatory words, if you do at all.
- *Don't overuse effects* – it's the first sign of an amateur. Look at most professional video material and it's just cut, cut, cut. For some reason, young journalists often don't seem to be able to get their heads round this and think there should be wacky fonts and crazy transitions happening all the over the place. There doesn't. Just tell the story.
- *Movement in every edit* – I can't remember if I read this somewhere or if someone told me during one of the many hours I've spent sitting in an editing suite. But it's advice that's stuck with me – if you have the choice between two shots, choose the one with movement in it.
- *Pacing* – it sounds a bit fancy, but I like to think of an editing job as like creating a piece of music (and I'm not a songwriter, so this isn't some feeble attempt to pretend I'm a rock star). Different pieces have different rhythms,

that should become apparent as you're making them. One package might be like a march – beat, beat, beat, beat of a drum. Another artefact might be more jazzy – a little Dizzy Gillespie here, some Charlie Parker there. The thing you're working on should hopefully sit up and show itself to be the piece of music it needs to be. Rhythm is absolutely vital.

- *Rewriting the story, again* – George Lucas' favourite part of the film-making process was editing. It gave him a chance to make the movie for a third time, after scriptwriting and production. You may not be making the next Star Wars film, but you can adopt the same mentality. Sitting in the edit suite is where you can decide what you want to make – based on the material you have and your creativity. Don't be afraid to experiment and explore how best to tell your story. And indeed *which* story is the best one to tell.

Equipment

It's not about the equipment you have. A student came to me recently asking about how he was going to shoot his 30-minute documentary 'flat', a technical term about the settings you utilise on the camera. I asked him if he'd ever made a documentary before. I asked him who his interviewees were and whether he had a sense of the narrative or the structure he might be employing. He didn't have good answers to any of these questions (it was a big "no" to the first). This illustrates a good point. If you're a journalist and you're going to be using kit like cameras and such, then none of it matters if what you produce doesn't have a strong story and good content. Audiences have become more forgiving of dodgy visuals recently – there are poor-visual-quality Skype interviews from the Middle East on the news all the time – but what they still want is the video they're watching to be informative and/or entertaining.

That's not to say you should ignore how your material looks or sounds. Far from it. A well-executed piece of technical journalism can demonstrate the difference between a professional and amateur. But *nothing* matters if the story is a dud.

To ensure that you achieve what you want to achieve in audio and video, it's up to you to research what best suits your situation. Will a smartphone be enough? Should you get a radio mic or a USB rifle one? Is it worth investing in a soundboard? How many stars did that tripod get on Reevoo? These are all questions you need to ask in different situations, weighing up the circumstances in each case. A book trying to answer them would run to 1000 pages, infuriate half its readers and be obsolete the day after it was written. But whenever you pick up a microphone, push your hand through the strap of a video camera or push up the fader, think about the context of what you are doing and how best your goal is served by which tools.

Ten top tips – multimedia

1. Remember you're a journalist, not a technician. Having a load of multimedia skills is great, but if you've got enough to do your job as a hack, then that's enough. At least to start with.

2. Teach yourself how to take good photos. It'll improve your journalistic eye, make you better at shooting video and put you in with the chance of earning extra money by selling your pictures to an agency that can syndicate them. This also means teaching yourself how to use Photoshop, which is an invaluable tool if you're working online in particular, where you'll mostly be expected to crop and edit the pictures you use.

3. You generally earn more as a cameraperson or technical/operations-type person. Just to let you know.

4. You don't necessarily need a 4K camera to shoot a piece, but making lower-end equipment look really good requires a bit more skill and panache. So learn it, or use a better camera than your iPhone.

5. Explore the app store on your phone. There are some brilliant, innovative things on there which will help your work to stand out. And make you look more hireable to older editors.

6. Think about different ways to present material. I highly recommend David McCandless' TED talk about data visualisation. It's from all the way back in 2010 and is still remarkable, so think how much better things are now.

7. If you're shooting video, don't settle for less. Boss your shoot and make sure the visuals are what you want.

8. Please, please, please use a proper microphone when recording video. And test audio levels if you're shooting an interview.

9. Think about where your multimedia is going to end up. Should it be shot vertically? Do you need to edit it with subtitles? Consider your audience (not the first time that phrase has been used in these lists of tips).

10. Yes, there's still plenty of life in podcasts. It's just harder to break through. So think about strategy/funding/structure/marketing before you start a new one.

TIM MUFFETT – REPORTER, *BBC BREAKFAST*

What would you say to a person looking to break into your profession right now?

The TV news industry has changed dramatically since 1994 when I started working in it. But some fundamental points remain valid. Be prepared to work for nothing, or next to nothing, for a certain period of time at the start. Easier said than done for sure, but without the most monumental piece of luck, you will not walk into a well-paid job straight from college.

Having undertaken numerous unpaid stints whilst at school and university, my starting salary was £8,000 a year as a researcher for a long defunct cable tv station called Channel One (try Wikipedia). Like waiting for a bus and two coming at once, I had simultaneously been offered almost twice as much to work for a media-buying department of an advertising agency. I stuck to what I wanted to do and never regretted it.

The opportunities to gain experience were incredible. I became a multi-skilled video journalist within six months (Channel One was the first British outlet to use VJs – long before the BBC). I even managed to interview Tom Cruise at the premiere of *Jerry Maguire* with a large Betacam TV camera on my shoulder and a microphone thrust forward in my outstretched hand – whilst the more established camera crews looked on somewhat bemused.

At the time I must have looked most peculiar – even Tom was incredulous ("Hey where's your cameraman?") but I was doing what I wanted to do – a great feeling – and have been lucky enough to do so ever since.

Circuitously, many local stations around the UK have been launched in the last few years. I would be contacting them and offering to tell local stories. Or get in touch with a local paper and offer to provide a report for their website. It is unlikely they will turn down free content. If they have equipment you can use, great – if not, film and edit it on your phone.

Get some pieces broadcast or uploaded, and then start badgering your regional BBC or ITV newsroom. They are likely to welcome your enthusiasm.

What are the three most important things you need as an entertainment broadcast journalist?

1. Have a genuine desire to learn about random things. Each week I become a 'mini expert' on a topic I would never have predicted the week, or even the day, before. That enthusiasm (hopefully!) comes across.
2. Get on with people. In my job, you dip into strangers' lives on a daily basis. It depends on the report, but if you want them to share, say, a personal story on camera, it helps hugely if you come across as someone who at least empathises with their situation. Don't try too hard to be everybody's best mate, but putting yourself in someone else's shoes is a good idea, I think.
3. Be self-confident, but not too cocky or arrogant. (Piers Morgan and others might disagree.)

What do you know now that you wish you'd known when you became a broadcast journalist?

New technology continually changes the industry. For example, I never believed videocassettes would disappear – how could that ever happen? Not everything new is successful (3D TV anyone?), but be aware of where things are heading and the impact it could have on your job. Try and embrace it.

How do you see the future of your profession and what might a young person need to know moving forward?

Staff (i.e. permanent) jobs will become increasingly rare, and budgets are only getting smaller. But on the plus side, I have a broadcast-quality camera in my pocket and the concept of an editing suite – once-mysterious rooms where machines costing tens of thousands of pounds could only be operated by a select few – has changed. Those suites still exist, as do talented editors, but the MacBook on which I am typing this at home was used the other day to edit a report that aired on BBC One. Be multiskilled and embrace technology.

I also regret not speaking another language – not a problem in some countries, of course, but it limits opportunities elsewhere. So another recommendation would be to learn a language if possible or if you have the basics from school, brush up to conversational standard. It opens up an array of opportunities – at the BBC, jobs are often advertised which need language skills – and they are often the hardest to fill. It is a skill most don't have.

What's the best thing about your job?

It's varied, mentally stimulating and days which I might consider 'a bit dull' are, by comparison to a lot of jobs, still very, very interesting.

What are your favourite moments you've had in your job?

Broadcasting live from the Oscars after-party. Exciting, fascinating, adrenaline-fuelled – something many would pay to do and yet part of my job.

From 2000 to 2002 I was Los Angeles Correspondent for Sky News and Sky Movies. At the time, Sky didn't have a presence on the west coast of the USA, and I was lucky enough to be offered the job.

Working abroad is a fantastic experience and opportunity, especially for a reporter. A different culture, a different context for the stories you are covering. There are of course challenges – not least the distance from friends and family – but in terms of life experience I would certainly recommend it.

Issues such as work visas can pose a challenge outside of Europe. I was fortunate in that Sky sorted this for me, but even if you are freelance, the backing of a regular client can help.

(Interview with author, 2017)

9

LAW AND ETHICS

This is such a difficult area. Partly because it can change – witness the Defamation Act 2013, which redefined how defamation in the media is argued (more on that in a moment) – and also because this is a book for journalists, not for lawyers. However, as a journalist, especially one working in a potentially litigious area like entertainment, it behoves a young creative to at least grasp the basic concepts of what you can and can't do and how one should act. The latter is particularly problematic because ethics are essentially the same as one's morals. It could be argued that ethics are morals for professional purposes. Is it 'okay' to gatecrash celebrity weddings and if asked who you are, to smile and say you are a friend of the bride from Weight Watchers, like Sharon Marshall attests she did in her book, *Tabloid Girl* (2010)? Or, as she also mentions, to give folding money to child soap stars so they come and talk to you at a premiere? Or to do as one of Marshall's colleagues has done and show up, wearing a doctor's coat, at the door of a celebrity's father who is dying of terminal cancer and then ask him what his famous son thinks about the illness? Placed out of context here, it sounds abhorrent, but readers still read the resulting stories, so to what extent can we judge?

What is true is that there's been a sea change in attitudes to the media over the past 20 years: the Leveson Inquiry, the closure of the *News of the World* in 2011, the outcry over paparazzi chasing Princess Diana to her death in 1997, superinjunctions to block revelations about the private lives of famous individuals and the explosion of the Internet and social media have all contributed to, one could argue, the current distrust in the mainstream media and the railing against so-called 'fake news' (copyright: President Trump). This isn't supposed to be a treatise about press freedom or the tabloidisation of the media, though it is this more sceptical, post-Leveson environment within which you will be participating. Keeble points out that a March 1999 editorial in the *Independent* actually argued an increase in the amount of coverage of popular culture within the media, including broadsheets, makes "cultural life more open and democratic" (Keeble, 2008).

Instead, this chapter attempts to highlight some of the most important things legally and ethically that you will need to know as you begin your career. What you will discover is that in a 24-hour news culture, you'll likely be expected to produce more content more quickly than any people who came before you while, at the same time, being under more scrutiny. Just because you're working in the supposedly glamorous and lightweight world of showbiz doesn't make it any less pressured or difficult to navigate (Forrest, 2013).

Leveson

With hearings held during 2011 and 2012 and with a report printed on 29 November 2012, Lord Justice Leveson's inquiry into the culture, practices and ethics of the press – precipitated by the phone hacking scandal and extended to explore accusations of too-cosy relationships between the press and public officials and more – was a landmark moment for the modern media in the UK. The efficacy of the inquiry itself is questionable – the finished report featured only a tiny mention of online media, and glossy magazines got an easy ride – but there's no doubt that Leveson's investigation impacted attitudes from then on. There were nine months of oral hearings, 300 people or groups gave written statements, and 337 people appeared and gave evidence in person. While Leveson argued in his report that the press was crucial to maintaining a free country and healthy democracy, he also admitted

> there have been far too many occasions over the last decade and more ... when these responsibilities, on which the public so heavily rely, have simply been ignored. There have been too many times when, chasing the story, part of the press have acted as if its own code, which it wrote, simply did not exist.
>
> *(Leveson, 2012)*

Leveson was faced with a lot of difficulties. Mainly it was a media that didn't want to believe what they'd done was wrong. Editors came to give evidence convinced they were acting honourably and there was no rot. Sharon Marshall, in her written evidence to the inquiry, explained how on her first day at *News of the World*, she was given a staff handbook which contained the Press Complaints Commission (PCC) Code of Practice. Describing the incident that she had recounted in her memoir about a colleague falsely dressing as a doctor, she wrote, "I only have anecdotal evidence of this and the precise details of the tale as described in the book should be seen as a dramatization." (Marshall, 2011)

Personally, I felt that Leveson conflated too many issues and didn't really tackle any of them truly effectively. But while many journalists might argue that – like the bankers who have returned to their gambling, irresponsible methods despite the world still reeling from the effects of the global financial crisis caused by this very behaviour – journalists haven't changed their ways all that much, Leveson remains a very easy marker for what constitutes erratic journalism and how much more closely the media is being examined by the outside world. Some of his recom-mendations are integrated into this chapter, but for a lengthier and more detailed look at them, the report is readily available on the UK government website.

The regulators

What Justice Leveson was clear about was the complete failure of the Press Com-plaints Commission and the need for reform in press regulation. Criticising it for a lack of independence – "in practice, the PCC has proved itself to be aligned with the interests of the press," he wrote – the judge was also loathe to ratify proposals raised during the inquiry for a new body. Lord Black of Brentwood pitched an idea for a new outfit which "would involve continuation [of] the complaints handling role of the PCC but place it alongside the creation of a separate arm of the regulator with powers to investigate serious or systemic failures and levy pro-portionate fines where appropriate" (Leveson, 2012). But Leveson wasn't convinced, saying that this still didn't "meet the test of independence" and that the new body "must represent the interests of the public as well as the press".

This caused a lot of consternation amongst media bigwigs and led to a complicated debate, mostly driven by self-interest, about what the regulator should look like and who would be a part of it. The result was two new bodies – the Independent Press Standards Organisation (IPSO) and IMPRESS, which describes itself as "the first truly independent press regulator in the UK". The former, formed in September 2014, is seen as the true spiritual heir of the PCC and is the one to which most media outlets have signed up (both the *Guardian* and the *Financial Times* have rejected it, preferring their own system of regulation). It has a 12-strong board made up predominantly of people outside the media.

Opponents of IPSO, including the National Union of Journalists, argue it's not independent and is merely a repackaged version of the PCC. IMPRESS has been backed by those pushing for press reform. Approved in October 2016 and accredited by the Press Recognition Panel (PRP), it currently has only a few signees, mostly hyperlocal press. Its critics are vociferous in their disapproval, perceiving it to be government-backed (the PRP was created and received a royal charter in the wake of Leveson). Evan Harris, a joint executive director of campaign group Hacked Off, told the BBC,

> The days of failed industry-controlled regulators like the PCC and its sham replacement IPSO are numbered. This decision makes Impress the only reg-ulator which the public, readers and victims of press abuse can trust to regulate newspapers and safeguard freedom of the press, while offering redress when they get things wrong.
>
> *(Cited in BBC, 2016)*

So why does this matter to you? Well, the political backstory doesn't really. Until you rise to management level, it's unlikely you'll be dealing with that directly.

However, if you get a job in the print or online journalism industry, your outlet might well be a member of one of these groups and as a journalist you always need to be across the legal framework within which your work sits. Your work will be subject to scrutiny by them should your outlet come under review. Mostly the guidelines are common sense, but you should read them and understand how they operate. Above all, you need to realise that there are now structures in place should people want to seek redress against something you've written. Both IPSO and IMPRESS have ostensibly been created to represent the public rather than the press. To make the complaints system more transparent and fair (commentators can continue to argue about whether this is true) while, particularly in the case of IMPRESS, installing a safe whistle-blowing system for journalists who think that their employers are engaging in unethical or illegal practices. The spectre of press regulation floats above all hacks, including the entertainment desk – don't be ignorant of it. An editor's code of practice, including everything from the use of subterfuge to harassment and the reporting of suicide, can be found on the IPSO website. I suggest you study it.

A quick word here about the broadcast regulator, known as Ofcom. Created in 2001, the Office of Communications now also looks after the BBC as well as video-on-demand services, which it oversees using its Broadcasting Code. It's generally stronger than its self-regulated counterparts, able to impose huge, punitive fines like the £5 million it made ITV pay in 2008 for misleading its audience surrounding competitive phone-ins. The rise of online video and streaming has challenged Ofcom – Sky and Channel 4's catch-up services come under its remit, as does Amazon Prime Video, but Netflix and more importantly YouTube do not as they are essentially 'broadcast' from the US. So for those of you producing content on the last two, the Broadcasting Code might not strictly apply to you. *But* … as journalists you should still abide by it. These services and their equivalents still fall under the legal framework of this country, and YouTube itself has clearly delineated community guidelines that don't immunise you from anything. So if you are creating entrepreneurial video content online, imagine you are a broadcaster, with all the rules and regulations that entails. That doesn't mean you can't still be bold or innovative or daring. It's not about censoring you. What it is about is protecting you – and your audience – from unfairness and harm. And that's not something to ignore. Again, I refer you to Ofcom's website for a full list of the guidelines.

Privacy

It's clear, writes Barnes, that for "rules that govern stalking, defamation and invasions of privacy carried out by paparazzi on behalf of public media outlets, the most striking difference [from the US] is evident in the European Union's concerted efforts to 'get it right'" (Barnes, 2010).

Parts of the Human Rights Act 1998 focused on protecting privacy, and the Council of European Parliamentary Assembly has tried to educate young journalists about the importance of privacy and how that manifests itself within a media environment (Barnes, 2010). Clearly the phone hacking scandal was a primary case study about privacy, and its repercussions are ongoing and wide-ranging at the time of writing. Millions of pounds have been paid out in settlements, people have gone to prison, and hugely profitable newspapers have closed as a result of illegal invasions into people's privacy. I would say celebrities – and certainly there are dozens of famous people who've been wronged – but this also includes people who became public without intending to (most horrifically, the murdered schoolgirl Milly Dowler).

But setting aside the illegal behaviour of media outlets, where does the concept of privacy begin and end? It's important to recognise that what you consider the concept of privacy to mean and the legal concept are two completely different things. While we all understand what privacy means in a personal context, there is currently no one official UK law governing invasion of privacy. Rather the Human Rights Act 1988 incorporates articles from the European Convention on Human Rights, specifically Article 8, which states, "Everyone has the right to respect for his private and family life, his home and his correspondence." However, as Contact Law rightly points out, when it comes to privacy from media intrusion, Article 8 can conflict "with another [article] – freedom of expression – which is commonly used as a defence by the press in high-profile privacy law cases" (Contact Law, n.d.). Because it's become part of the Human Rights Act, Brexit won't change this moving forward, although that might change depending on whether the government ever decides to follow through on the long-discussed British Bill of Rights (Practical Law, n.d.). Unsurprisingly, media editors (particularly tabloid ones like the *Daily Mail*'s Paul Dacre) are generally against the idea of a privacy law, while others have argued that if revealing the details of someone's private life means that the media also has the capacity to weed out, say, governmental corruption without fear of being suppressed by a privacy law, then that's a price worth paying. (Those whose lives are turned upside down in full view of the public would probably disagree.)

In other words, not everyone is 'fair game' to be written about in forensic detail. The Data Protection Act 1998 is also important to mention here, relating as it does to how companies are able to use personal data both privately and publicly (see the UK government website for the list of its rules in full). Journalists should always ask themselves: is it in the public interest? Be particularly careful when the privacy of children is involved. And remember, this is a very grey area, even when it seems otherwise. Footballer Ashley Cole settled with various newspapers in 2009, having brought a claim for invasion of privacy against them after they published details about his extra-marital affairs. Cole argued that despite being a famous footballer, he didn't hold public office and thus information about his sex life was not in the public interest. The newspapers replied by saying that he was a public figure and didn't have a reasonable expectation of privacy in this case, further arguing that by selling his marriage to Cheryl (then Cole) to magazines, he had essentially opened his romantic life to the public domain.

The moral here? Separate the person from the work. When people put their work in front of the world for public consumption, they are eschewing the right to privacy for what they've created, not necessarily for themselves. And as Cole proves, the concept of 'fame' can be argued according to circumstance. Just because someone is well known, that doesn't make them famous. This feels particularly true in a broad and popular culture where someone might be iconic to a certain section of society (YouTube stars, for example) and not to the audience at large. How might an Internet celebrity be perceived were they to launch a similar privacy case? The answer is that it would have to be tested in court.

THE LAWYER'S VIEW

Joel Rapaport is a media lawyer as well as a producer and performer for the online children's series *Hoot Quarters*, so he understands both the creative and the legal side of making content.

Do you think media outlets are scared by threat of lawyers?

> I suspect this is highly dependent on the outlet. I am sure that the Hulk Hogan/Gawker case (in March 2016, a US jury found in favour of the former wrestler who had sued the gossip site after they published a sex tape featuring him, awarding him over £100 million in damages, which meant Gawker declared bankruptcy) has made folks in this industry at least think twice about what they publish and where the 'legal' line is. However, the particular story that lead to that dispute is probably something that would not even cross the desks of a lot of editors, or if it did, would quickly be determined not something they would cover.

How do you see the relationship between the entertainment media and lawyers?

> Every party has a lawyer, and except for who is paying their bills, there is usually not too much that divides the lawyers on one side from those on the other. It may be that some primarily represent one type of party verses another type of party, but they are all studying the same laws – they are just applying them in different ways. Thus, on one hand the entertainment media needs lawyers – hopefully to advise them wisely where the line of what is legal and what is not likely is – and on the other side there will always be lawyers (on behalf of – in this set-up – parties aggrieved by the press) seeking to push that line further and further towards the media (or any party).

Are celebrities especially litigious nowadays do you think, with the media?

> I will say most people/entities, in my experience, don't enjoy litigation. It is a process that is available to those that feel, and may have been, wronged in some ways.
>
> When asking a question like this, while it does not call for it, I think it is important to consider that celebrities would likely not be celebrities without

the media in the first place. Thus, just like the legal system provides a framework for people to seek damages for legal wrongs, the media industry is a framework for proliferating information – including that in an entertainment setting.

When I worked at a weekly magazine, it was more about threats – "We're watching you this week; don't talk about me." Have you seen or heard that kind of thing?

Not especially, but I am not really in the trenches so to speak on this issue. I would imagine that this is a much bigger issue at a weekly (if by this you mean the *National Enquirer*) than some other media outlets.

Do you feel the media is correctly regulated from a legal and ethical perspective right now?

This is a complicated question. I can't really say what is 'correct' from a legal standpoint except to say that it is whatever [the government] says it is. Though, attorneys usually make their money by arguing that two entirely different things are simultaneously 'correct'. From an ethical standpoint, this is probably harder. I don't know what the standards of journalistic ethics are. I can say I often read articles and think to myself "What benefit does this serve the public?" Though I often feel very similar about TV, film, music, etc … and it is not my place to make that determination either, except perhaps to make decisions as a consumer about whom I give my 'advertising' impressions. Further, I know enough to know that I do not represent the public at large, and I don't know what others deem valuable or of journalistic importance.

What should a young journalist watch out for, do you think, from a legal perspective? Not just "don't defame someone". I mean – what do you think are the legal minefields right now?

I think not defaming someone is certainly a good place to start, and trying to understand what the laws around that are. They are really not tremendously complicated when it comes to highly public figures. Thus, having an understanding of this at the start is important.

While it is difficult to stand up to a boss, especially just starting out in any career when you need to pay rent, trying to figure out what will be expected of you from the beginning going into a position and how much of a say you will have in the story is important to know. While difficult to say from the outside, maintaining your integrity, in the long run, is likely far more beneficial than the next pay cheque. It might also be worth asking about previous lawsuits (or doing some Google, PACER, Lexis searches – check out your local law library for access) to see if your potential employer has been brought up in cases and how they handled it. Further, ask in an interview what their policy is if a lawsuit is brought forth and if a demand is made. It is rare in my career that I have seen a plaintiff go after the little guy (i.e. reporter) when there was someone with deeper pockets involved.

On that topic, how do you see the legal overseeing of the Internet/social media progressing?

This is really a question for [government] and I suppose how effective various lobbying and advocacy efforts are in the future. Further, how cases are decided, which will set precedent in the future. [In the US], we have a new member of the Supreme Court and several members that are by no means young, thus there are bound to be changes and new interpretations to these laws as time passes and new issues come before them.

Defamation

Fundamental to every journalist is the law of defamation – also known as libel in print or slander if spoken – and making sure you don't break it. While some areas of media law will be less applicable to those working in the entertainment field, defamation is ever-present (Quinn, 2013). The Defamation Act 2013 fundamentally altered a lot of traditional rules around this concept, primarily attemping, as UK Parliament states, to "reform the law of defamation to ensure that a fair balance is struck between the right to freedom of expression and the protection of reputation" (UK Parliament, n.d.). Above all, it intended that potential claimants had to show that they had suffered or will suffer serious harm from what was written about them before they could sue for defamation. The Act itself states, "a statement is not defamatory unless its publication has caused or is likely to cause serious harm to the reputation of the claimant," adding, "For the purposes of this section, harm to the reputation of a body that trades for profit is not 'serious harm' unless it has caused or is likely to cause the body serious financial loss." (Defamation Act 2013, section 1) In other words, to allege something which "causes [the claimant] loss in their trade or profession, or causes a reasonable person to think worse of him, her or them" (Wikipedia, 2017).

I have never been officially sued (yet!), but I've come close a couple of times. Once was when I wrote an unauthorised biography of the physicist Professor Brian Cox. I sent an interview request to him just before the manuscript was to be handed in and received a cautionary letter from his legal team, making sure I understood they were looking closely at what I'd written in case there was anything defamatory in it (there wasn't, and Cox and I exchanged brief emails following publication alluding to me doing a solid job without specifically endorsing the product.) The second was while I was on the news desk at a weekly magazine involving a rock star and a former girlfriend who felt she'd been disparaged during an interview (which was actually bought in, but had my name attached to it, even though I didn't do it).

More common at my weekly was a circular letter from one of the top celebrity law firms at the beginning of a week (probably sent out to the other glossies at the same time), warning us that they were watching the press closely that week for any unfavourable mentions of their client. That usually pre-cipitated a moratorium on stories about that person for a while. But while we came close to the edge of defamation on occasion, especially when it came to famous women's bodies and whether they were "unhealthily thin or obese", outlets are very cautious about writing anything that could even be perceived as defamatory.

As per the Defamation Act 2013, there are legal defences to a charge of libel or slander. This might be that it was, shock horror, the truth, or that it was an honestly held opinion (these replaced justification and so-called fair comment). More murkily, it can be argued that the statement was in the public interest, which is potentially harder to prove. This is also a defence frequently turned to by media outlets, but it is fraught with problems, most notably whether something is genuinely in the public interest or whether it's just in the interest of the public. The latter is *not* a defence. Whereas US publications tend to lean on the First Amendment and make any defamation claim some kind of swingeing attack on that most sacred of constitutional artefacts, the UK doesn't have such protections.

For an entertainment journalist, this is pretty simple: (a) don't make up things about people; (b) read the above statements and make sure you aren't crossing any of those lines; and (c) don't think just because you say it idly in a tweet or you don't really mean it or you're just making a joke, you can't be found guilty of defamation. You only need to look at the 2017 libel judgement won by journalist and campaigner Jack Monroe against outspoken right-wing commentator Katie Hopkins to realise that.

Copyright

Okay, so this is a huge and unimaginably complex area of law I'm going to reduce rather embarrassingly down to some very basic truths which I believe are most important for those of you starting out in this industry. Why it's crucial we mention copyright here is because it's a facet of modern journalism which the young people I've encountered invariably get wrong and, more worryingly, come up with strange justifications or reasons for why they have acted the way they have. It's that kind of Chinese whispers approach to copyright infringement – "I heard that it was alright to …" – which threatens to cause damage.

- *Just because someone else has used something, doesn't mean you can.* As has been shown in this chapter, it's possible to sue multiple outlets for the same crime. So if you take something because someone else has and they are challenged about it, then the complainant can challenge you too.
- *Related to the above point,* if it's on YouTube, it doesn't mean it's copyright-free.
- *That means you can't just credit something and assume it's fine.* Some of the time that is enough to demonstrate you haven't plagiarised, but it's not a catch-all.
- *You can't copyright an idea.* If it's not codified in some way, then it's potentially fair game. This is why applicants for jobs often get annoyed when they're asked to submit pitches for a TV show or five feature pieces that would work for a certain magazine. While outright stealing in this capacity happens very infrequently, it can and does happen.
- *Be careful making any content about sport.* Video or photos from sports which are signed to lucrative rights deals is watched very, very carefully.
- *Copyright around material from social media and things like gifs is a moveable feast.* In my experience and at the time of writing, creating gifs has been fine, as has utilising material from Facebook and Twitter, as long as you credit where it comes from. But the law is evolving around this kind of digital work, so it won't necessarily stay like this forever.
- *Be careful with pictures!* This is someone's livelihood. Or it's owned by a large agency which charges for subscription. If you're searching on Google, use Creative Commons, or do an advanced search for a picture that can be reproduced elsewhere. Also, do your due diligence in trying to locate and get permission of copyright holders.

Ethics

What are ethics? Eek. Truthfully, it's an unanswerable question because it depends on so many variables – your moral compass, your belief system and what is expected from your employer. The Society of Professional Journalists in America lays out a one-page code, which includes guidelines that I would say pertain particularly to entertainment journalists. They include: "neither speed nor format excuses inaccuracy"; "never deliberately distort facts or context, including visual information"; "avoid pandering to lurid curiosity, even if others do"; "consider the long-term implications of the extended reach and permanence of publication"; "avoid conflicts of interest, real or perceived"; and "distinguish news from advertising and shun hybrids that blur the lines between the two". The irony is that the code insists at the bottom of the page that "It is not, nor can it be under the First Amendment, legally enforceable." And this is the difference between law and ethics. It's not about illegal practices like phone hacking, or defaming someone, it's about how a journalist goes about the business of their job. But how one navigates ethics does affect public trust in journalists as a group. There may be something of a moral panic about the state of the media, but it's true that surveys regularly place hacks at the bottom of the list of jobs with public credibility (Keeble, 2008). It's true too that in a 24-hour news age, there's pressure on journalists like never before. The frantic pace of entertainment news now means that it's incredibly difficult, especially with a reliance on more freelance staff and demands from management, to pursue the kinds of processes necessary to ensure information is accurate and contextualised. What's more, in a more fragile job market, a journalist is perhaps less likely to question their bosses if they are asked or it's suggested that they do something a little unethical (Keeble, 2008). "As a shift-worker you are not given any contractual rights as you are only hired for a 24-hour period on a day to day basis," submitted Sharon Marshall in her Leveson Inquiry witness statement, discussing her time working on the news desk at a tabloid newspaper.

> You must prove your worth each day or else face the fact that it is likely you will not be hired again at that newspaper. The pressure was not therefore from the Editor or the proprietors of the newspaper, but was more from a desire to continue working and to build up a reputation as a successful journalist ready to get taken on full time as a staff reporter.
>
> *(Marshall, 2011)*

Keeble highlights three ways that journalists can approach ethics. One is cynically – that is, you shouldn't have any as long as you are working inside the law. They will only cause roadblocks in the progression of your career. The second is relying on your own humanity. Do unto others … and all that. And then there's "the stress on professionalism", the notion that your behaviour is part of something bigger, more important and more long-lasting than you as an individual (Keeble, 2008). In reality, the latter two are inextricably linked – why would you adhere to professional standards if you didn't already have personal ones? There are, unfortunately, still too many journalists who abide by the first approach. One of their arguments is that the audience gets the journalism it deserves. We want to read about the more salacious aspects of celebrity, and we don't care whether a movie director or a multimillionaire pop star's latest output is eviscerated in carefree fashion. They're famous; they chose to do it; get used to it.

There are elements of truth in this. It can be infuriating when modern-day celebrities question the intrusion into their love lives. It's as if they've grown up in a parallel universe where *heat* wasn't published every week. Okay, I don't think anyone can fully comprehend what it's like to be famous until they are, but artists generally go into the profession with their eyes open. It's rare that there's an accidental movie star or someone who mistakenly sells out Wembley Stadium. They do so by practising their craft and generally also through seeking publicity. That said, just because people wanted to be famous, it doesn't mean you have unfettered licence to talk about them however you want. This also, I might add, applies from a legal perspective. Barnes writes,

> The very legal arguments that run amok in the United States (i.e. because celebrities enjoy the public's adoration, they must be exempt from the general protection of the law as they possess enhanced means for setting the record straight and countering false charges) are often rejected throughout Europe.
>
> *(Barnes, 2010)*

Ten top tips – The law and ethics of entertainment journalism

1. Don't be a dick.
2. It's entirely likely you'll be sued, or threatened with it, at one point in your career. Don't panic (if you know you did what you did in good faith).
3. If you work at a big company, they'll probably have a lawyer on retainer. Utilise them by all means, but don't rely on them solely. If the s**t hits the fan, you'll be the one who takes the heat.
4. Read the guidelines and have a copy of MacNae's by your desk. Better to be safe than sorry.
5. As the phone hacking prosecutions taught us, the argument that everyone else was doing it doesn't always work. Be your own person even if you're feeling pressure from above. If you are feeling pressure, speak to someone you trust about it.
6. The Leveson Inquiry seemed to suggest it was only the tabloid papers involved in wrongdoing. I can attest that this wasn't the case. It can happen anywhere.
7. No, it's not okay to just take anything you want from the Internet. The likelihood of this coming back to bite you will only increase moving forward as the legalities around online copyright are configured and refined. Get out of the habit now.
8. The law is a moving beast. Always keep on top of the latest developments.
9. Certain people do need to be held to account, even treated in an adversarial way, but always think about the context within which you are reporting and the impact your content will have.
10. Breaking the law on the Internet is just as bad as doing it on telly or in print. Just ask Katie Hopkins.

ALEX STANGER – BROADCAST JOURNALIST/REPORTER, BBC

What would you say to a person looking to break into your profession right now?

> It is really important to be able to work across all genres and perhaps perfect one. Also, you don't have to be an expert at everything, but it helps to have one specific field you are interested in like film or music.

What are the three most important things you need in your job?

1. I have worked as a reporter, a presenter and now a video journalist, and I think one of the most important things is you always have to adapt because the industry is always changing. When I was a presenter, I didn't want to step behind the camera at all, but now I love making my films from start to finish knowing it is all my own work.
2. I think charm coupled with perseverance goes a long way in getting a good story – never underestimate just how important being nice is. It means people choose to work with you and may be more willing to give you an exclusive.
3. Stamina – you really need it. If you are covering something like the Cannes film festival, you will be expected at a screening at 8.30 a.m., then interviews/press conferences for the rest of the day (lugging your kit from one venue to another), then various red carpets in the evening whilst filing and editing pieces as you go. Cannes, the Oscars and various awards shows have made some of the best moments in my career, but in reality lugging kit and tearing your hair out when you can't feed stuff back into London before a crucial deadline can shake the nerves of any reporter. I would say having good stamina is one way to get through it all.

What do you know now that you wish you'd known when you became an entertainment reporter?

I have loved being an entertainment reporter, but be warned it is very tricky to move jobs from entertainment into other fields. Also, you'll have a great, exciting, fun-packed career, but it is highly unlikely you will ever make a fortune!

How do you see the future of your profession and what might a young person need to know moving forward?

I think the future is great for entertainment journalism as more and more people are using it as a form of entertainment in itself – when they want to unwind, they will look at the entertainment pages of a website rather than the news headlines. Just make sure that you are across every genre, especially video. As social media is the way most people are now getting their news, video is best placed here. You have to figure out a way to make imaginative and striking content that people want to share – this is very different to the way I used to work.

What's the best thing about your job?

I still look forward to going to work! Also, I'm now being asked to be much more creative than ever before, which is a great challenge. I've met some really amazing people doing what I do and made lifelong friends with the people I have worked with. I've also travelled across the world reporting and presenting. It has been amazing.

Tell us about your favourite moments in your job?

Travelling for assignments and living in Los Angeles have definitely been highlights of my career. On that note, always get to the airport early when travelling with kit! It takes ages to check in, and I have had to run across far too many airports to make flights (and missed a few as well). [I've loved] getting exclusive access to things which have made great reports – mostly these have come about because when I get an idea I don't give up on it. It doesn't always work out, but I always know I tried extra hard to get it. I also enjoy being put higher up the red carpet. This usually comes about when the programme you are working on becomes more popular, or it could be because a PR knows and trusts you. PRs are not the enemy; they are there to work alongside. You don't always have to tow their line, but if you are honest and upfront, then you should be able to form a good working relationship, which can be crucial in the long term.

(Interview with author, 2017)

10

SELLING AS A FREELANCE

The rise of the so-called gig economy has reached its fingers into the world of journalism. While there are still lots of staff jobs, those starting out may well find themselves in what people call a portfolio career, working here and there and selling bits and bobs to make ends meet before you build up enough credit to get a full-time position. Of course, there are also those who never wish to sit behind a desk in an office, who'd prefer to be their own boss (after a fashion since you're still relying on someone to buy your material in order to pay your rent) and dip in and out of different outlets by working for them as a freelancer.

I would suggest that initially you try and get a staff job, with freelancing coming later. That way, you've built up contacts over a number of years and are more set before throwing yourself into uncertainty. Of course, the way the industry is now, you might not have a choice. Wherever and however you end up doing your journalism, despite what the naysayers argue, content is now king. If you have the right attitude and correct approach, you should be able to make it work.

Ideas

I covered this in Chapter 1 so I won't go into it in detail here, but it's an unavoidable fact that if you're a freelancer, you'll need to generate lots of potential story ideas … all the time. The main thing to remember is to try and think more cleverly about the most obvious things – that doesn't mean avoiding the main stories per se, but try and find a unique way into that story that works as something an outlet will chime with but also that you'll be able to deliver. When I worked in TV development, there was a running joke amongst channel commissioners about Mondays being the supplements day. In other words, people who worked for production companies got the weekend newspapers and then pitched something related to a trend written about in one of the many sections in those papers – a series making dishes which adhered to some new fad diet, a reality show about a neophyte Instagram fashion maven. That's the kind of obvious stuff you want to stay away from. Remember too that if you're just starting out, you're not going to be writing the centre-page spread about the Hollywood A-list star with a new movie out. They've got plenty of high-profile writers they know already who will be assigned that job. But maybe you can supplement it in some way with a spin-off from that or provide a possible sidebar idea which will complement it. Either way, if you're freelancing, you need to remind yourself that generation of ideas needs to be constant and innovative. Days when you're not thinking of possible content are days when you're not getting paid.

Twelve golden rules of freelancing

1. Research seems to be a frequent theme throughout this book, as well it should, but it's definitely applicable here. I'm not suggesting you do some kind of background check on the outlet you're pitching to, or indeed the editor/commissioner you are approaching, but knowledge is power. Read the outlet that you want to pitch to – not just the most recent issue or the current home page, but rather embed yourself in it. This should go hand in hand with your general reading schedule anyway. The kinds of places I love to pitch to feature the kinds of things I love to read, watch or listen to. But this is especially important if you've got an idea for something outside your wheelhouse. When I started writing real-life stories for women's tabloids, I had never read one of them. My local newsagent was pleased by a large magazine purchase which put me in the headspace of those editors and that audience. You may not get house style down pat straightaway, but at least you shouldn't look foolish.

2. This sounds defeatist, but there will be places which will simply never take a story from you because of who you are. This runs counter-intuitive to my argument that if you've got the right story, then editors will want it. But the fact of the matter is, I highly doubt I'll ever write something for *Vogue*. Even though I have interviewed women who've appeared in the magazine before for other places, the kind of specific knowledge you need to write a *Vogue* profile is something I don't have. It could be acquired. If early on you decide that *Vogue* is really who you want to write for, then do everything in your power to get a handle on the level of technical fashion savvy you need. Nevertheless, I think there is such a thing as choosing the incorrect outlet for *you*.

3. Don't apologise for pitching. This is something I've always been terrible at, although it's improved since I got older and wiser. Get it into your head that you are doing them a favour by reaching out. Yes you want them to commission your idea, but you don't have to feel like you're imposing on their magnificent life to pitch it. Journalists are busy, but they're not *that* busy, however much they like to say otherwise. If you're confident in your idea and you think it deserves to be seen, say so. By saying how sorry you are to

be taking up their valuable time, you're automatically sewing doubt in their minds that the idea has worth. Be proud of what you're sending them.

4. If an editor has notes on your piece after you've submitted it, don't be surprised. I always marvel at the way great editors completely understand their audience and know exactly how to sell the content to them. There is no such thing as the perfect piece. Don't get upset if you're asked to rewrite something or tweak it a little bit. It only means that the editor cares enough about his or her product to make it the best it can be, which is a good thing. Of course, it's important to learn from how and what you're asked to redo. Make sure you properly read the feedback and figure out why you've been asked to make the changes. Still, it'll probably happen for the rest of your career, so get used to it.

5. Do it on time and how you've been asked. If you've been told to submit 700 words by next Tuesday, that doesn't mean you can write 1000 by Wednesday (submitting it before deadline is fine, but I don't know many journalists for whom that's a normality). A friend of mine used to be a sub at *GQ* and always marvelled at how their 'star' interviewer wrote double the amount he was told to and then got furious when my mate had to cut it down to the required length. As a journalist, you're in service to the outlet you're creating content for. If you've got a half-hour television slot, you wouldn't submit an hour-long documentary, right? The advent of YouTube and podcasts in the broadcast sphere has meant that sometimes sticking to time isn't quite as crucial. And the Internet has meant that, in theory, if you're writing for online then you don't have to write so that you can fit a half-page ad in the corner of your double-page spread. But there's nothing more infuriating to a commissioning editor than if you haven't abided by their request. Yes, you may have infinite scroll, but if they wanted 500 words, then give them it.

6. 'Solutions journalism' – what can you do that will make an editor's life easier? (See below for an editor agreeing with this point.) An editor is basically trying to solve a jigsaw puzzle – fill a magazine or a television schedule or a home page or whatever with content that their audience will love and share. Think how you can fit together one or more of those pieces. What they definitely don't want is you causing them to ask any more questions.

7. Keep your pitch short. My rule of thumb is to imagine that when it arrives in an editor's inbox, I don't want them to have to use that little scroll wheel to read it. So basically I'm talking about, what, ten lines maximum? If you can't sum up why what you're pitching is great in that time, it's not a good enough idea. If they want to talk about it further and ask you to provide more information, that's when you can be more verbose. But at the start, think about what the headline/sell would be (particularly if it's online) and why the outlet in question needs to have it right now.

8. Don't be too formal. This isn't an essay. It's not an invitation to the White House. You're both people. Okay, so don't start the email with, "Alright

mate, got an idea ya might like"; but one of the ways a commissioner will judge whether you're the kind of person they'd like to buy something from will be by reading your email. So don't be too familiar, but don't make it feel like a circular from Clarence House either.

9. Remember that freelancing is a business. You may have wanted to become a journalist specifically because you didn't like all the people at university who ended up becoming management consultants and lawyers. But it's crucial to remind yourself you are the CEO of You Inc. That means you need to approach it professionally and carefully and think about workflows and all that kind of stuff that seems anathema to a lot of journos. Trust me – the ones who are clever about this and take it seriously are always the most successful.

10. Prepare yourself for the roller coaster. A journalism colleague contacted me one New Year's Eve and told me he'd just lost a £30,000 a year contract. One phone call and all that money gone. It's happened to me too. I've gone through periods of plenty and then two emails and a "I'm sorry, but …" meeting later and I've lost a huge chunk of income. Budgets are getting squeezed, a company gets taken over, someone you know leaves the place you work for and suddenly the money doesn't seem to be there any more. This is incredibly frustrating, but it's just the way it is now. There will be other opportunities, other avenues, if you just work hard.

11. Think about how you might supply to different outlets at the same time. This can be difficult and you don't want to upset any of your clients. And it won't work for every job or story that you do. But it's a way to earn a bit more money – say, write a more generic feature about a band for one outlet and then sell a couple of juicy, perhaps slightly differently angled quotes to the showbiz pages of a newspaper. You'll probably want to wait until you've got a decent relationship with the PR before attempting this, but as long as you're not putting out something negative, then most of the time the publicists realise it's all good promotion. There are news agencies who specialise in this kind of thing and who you can approach. Or you can simply phone up the tip line of a news desk and say you've got something for them. It might also mean that you'll need to tackle something like a junket a bit differently. I've had it where I'm asking film-specific questions for one job and then had to slip in a couple of parenting questions at the end of the interview. As long as you're above board with the PR, it's a good source of potential revenue.

12. If they say yes, ask again – quickly. Once you've established a rapport with someone you want to sell to, then come up with something else good as soon as possible and send it to them (though make sure it really is good and not just whatever you have lying around). As Ferris Bueller once said, "Life moves pretty fast." That includes the world of journalism. If someone's given you an in, then you need to make sure the door doesn't close before you get the chance to properly wedge your feet in there.

ROSIE NIXON – EDITOR-IN-CHIEF, *HELLO!*

What would you say to a person looking to break into your profession right now?

> Just go for it. It is undeniable that the world of journalism has gone through incredible changes in recent years in terms of technology and the way stories are presented across a multitude of platforms, but at the heart of everything we do are good stories – and we will always need genuine, fantastic content.
>
> Develop a 'voice' and a specialism with your writing and target that genre of publication. This is an incredible career with wonderful opportunities and the possibility of making a real difference in the world – if you are passionate and knowledgeable about your work, it will show.

What are the three most important things you need as an editor?

1. My contacts book. My position at *HELLO!* is reliant on my contacts within the industry, which have been built up over the 18 years I have worked as a magazine journalist. As we regularly feature the weddings or first baby photos of people in the public eye, I am regularly handling confidential or sensitive information, and the trust I have with our subjects is imperative. I am really proud and protective of the fact *HELLO!* works hand in hand with personalities to achieve such unique access.
2. A passion for the role. Being editor-in-chief across a brand like *HELLO!* requires dedication and stamina, and this would not be possible without a love for what I do. Mine is not a nine-to-five job. News stories can break at any time of day or night and the team will look to me for guidance. But the fast pace and the fact no two days are ever the same is exhilarating and what drives me to work each day – there isn't time to become bored!
3. Decisiveness. When there is discussion about whether to buy a set of paparazzi photos, the angle for a news story or a choice between images for the front cover, my role demands decisiveness. There is a huge responsibility in being the final decision maker; it is also essential for the practical reason that we have tight production deadlines to hit each week, so my team need to feel they have clear direction. Having worked at *HELLO!* for nine years now, I am practised at instinctively knowing what is right for our brand, and I have a deep understanding of what our readers – and commercial partners – expect from us. I also take my moral obligation as an editor very seriously.

What do you know now that you wish you'd known when you became a showbiz journalist and then subsequently an editor?

How quickly the impact of online reporting would affect our industry. The fact that everyone owning a mobile handset is effectively a photojournalist has changed the landscape for news reporting – showbiz stars can now break their own exclusives to their millions of followers around the globe in a matter of seconds and photos and videos emerge from the scene of big news events almost instantly, whereas only a few years ago, that wasn't the case. As such, it is harder than ever for journalists to land genuine exclusives, which makes our relationships with contacts even more precious.

How do you see the future of your profession and what might a young person need to know moving forward?

The integration of print with online and digital platforms is only going to increase, so journalists today must have a wide skill set. An understanding of the technical aspects of CMS [content management systems] and social media, as well as the ability to write accurate and sparkling copy, will stand you in good stead to turn your hand to whatever might be required.

(Interview with author, 2017)

Freelancing in the office

The traditional idea of what a freelance journalist does is someone who sits at home thinking up ideas, pitching them to editors and then writing/creating them. But it's worth pointing out that's not the only way you can be a freelance entertainment journalist.

The shrinking number of full-time staff members means a lot of outlets will recruit freelancers to come and do shifts in the office, sometimes for a day, sometimes for weeks or even months at a time. This can be a useful source of income – a lot of the places I've done this have subsequently hired me to write regular pieces for them because they know who I am and can put a face to the name. It also provides your life with some sort of structure, though if you are very successful at this, you may find yourself juggling several offers at a time (not necessarily a bad thing). Having lots of different places who pay you is vital for a financially viable freelance career. I know several people who do frequent subediting shifts at one place that pays them enough and gives them enough spare time to generate ideas and material independently. Those of you with design/CMS skills may also find that these are qualities prized for in-office work.

Remember as well that some jobs in entertainment journalism are almost always freelance ones. For example, most television jobs will be short, casual contracts, covering a particular show that you may be working on. Hopefully you'll be able to parlay that into something more long term, but if you work in broadcast, then you may find yourself hustling more than others, unless you are on staff as part of the in-house development team or are working on a long-running format.

The editor's view

You'll see longer interviews with them in the middle and at the end of this chapter, but I thought it would be useful to simply ask two top editors what they want from a freelancer. Here's what they said:

"Make sure you're contacting the correct person on staff," Suzy Cox, former editor of *heat* magazine, tells me.

> I know it sounds obvious, but call the editorial assistant first and find out who you need to be pitching your story to. If you send me a travel idea, it will probably get lost in my inbox, whereas *heat*'s Life Hacks editor will get back to you instantly. Think what you can offer that someone in the office can't. For example, do you have a really interesting take on a story, specialist knowledge, access to someone interesting? And for gawd's sake read the magazine you're pitching to. You should be able to tell me why your idea is uniquely right for *heat*.

She adds, "We always joke that our picture desk is a 'solutions-based department' but they are." She explains,

> If there's a problem – a picture I want is too expensive, a photographer has cancelled, we can't shoot a celeb until the morning we go to press – they always come to me with solutions and options instead of just the problem. Editors have so much going on at any one time – if you can help them solve issues before they become bigger ones, you'll go far!

"If there are two qualities a journalist must have, it is confidence and persistence," adds Rosie Nixon, Editor-in-Chief of *HELLO!*, explaining that being freelance for a publication might just give you the edge when they're looking for someone full-time. "You might just be in the right place when a vacancy becomes available," she says. "Submit ideas that are relevant – there is no point pitching a film review to a title that does not carry reviews; this will immediately make you look incompetent. Do your research and be focused when making an approach."

THE FREELANCER'S VIEW

Jill Foster worked as an editor at the *Mirror* and as an associate editor of the *Daily Mail*'s Femail section before going freelance a number of years ago. I asked her what she would say to a wannabe freelancer.

What does a young journalist just starting out as an entertainment/arts freelance need to be thinking about?

> Contacts, contacts, more contacts. Get out there. Meet people in these industries. Go to as many gigs/films/exhibitions/concerts as you can and keep in touch with the organisers. Stick around afterwards to meet the

people who made the films/music, etc. Be passionate about the industry and read up on and around it. Read books by these musicians/artists. Become familiar with the works of other journalists and see what they're saying about the same gigs/books/events. Learn from their reviews and interviews. Would you have done it differently? It's really about getting to know your subject at this early stage.

What are your five top tips for being a freelance journalist?

1.   Ideas are key – if you have no ideas, you have no copy. Keep a notebook of ideas, because they come to you at any moment.
2.   Keep your contacts warm. People move onwards and upwards, so keep in touch with people.
3.   Be nice. It costs nothing and even if your review of a particular film or interview with a certain person is scathing, be polite in person.
4.   Read the publications you're going to be pitching to. You'd be amazed at the amount of people who pitch blind – it's unprofessional.
5.   Keep all your receipts! You'll need them for your tax return!

What do people get wrong when trying to sell as a freelance?

Like I say, many don't even read the publication they're pitching to, so they get the tone wrong or they try to sell something completely unsuitable. I've had people try to pitch ideas which have run in the section that very week, so that's just rude. It shows a lack of respect for the person you're pitching to and hoping to get work from.

The boring nitty-gritty of being a freelancer

Being a freelancer requires a lot of organisation and some genuine thought before you undertake this role. For a start, you'll need a good portfolio website, showing off what you can do and what you've done already. The good news is that you don't have to be a professional coder now to create something that looks fantastic. I use Wix for my website, which is one of the drag-and-drop-style HTML5 products. Weebly and Squarespace are similar. Something like WordPress gives you a bit more flexibility, but I think it's always important to remember that you're not a designer – you're a journalist. Everything you're doing should be in service of achieving that goal (though if you're great at design and can show that off in your work, then it's another excellent string to your bow and a potentially lucrative revenue stream). It's like what I said in Chapter 8 on multimedia – I'm not a professional cameraman or editor, but I can do enough to fulfil my journalistic needs and make me hireable on that basis. I would suggest that you have the same mindset when it comes to your personal website.

Of course, this is slightly different if, for example, you're a YouTuber or are running an entertainment podcast. In that case, there is debate about the extent to which you need a website at all (though you probably do, as a home base), since it's feasible now to run all that through social media channels. Ultimately, it's up to you. And of course, you'll need to align your social media with your freelance goals. Talk on them about the kinds of stories you're interested in; demonstrate how your expertise about a particular topic permeates your entire cultural life.

Is it worth hiring a designer to make your website for you? I don't think so, though the maintenance can be a grind if you're busy. But as someone who should be curious about content creation and may even be working in an online environment, playing with and embracing the tools of the trade on something you own that is about promoting you will only make you better elsewhere in your job. You can never have too many areas of skill.

Tax. Yes, unfortunately, as long as you earn a certain amount of money doing it, you'll have to pay income tax on your freelance earnings. You still have to if you have a full-time PAYE job alongside doing freelance journalism. In the former case, becoming 'officially' self-employed is known in the trade as going Schedule D. I've never really known why and, you know what, I don't plan on finding out now. I just accept it and my responsibilities. Registering as a self-employed sole trader is something that you can do very easily on the HMRC website. The realities of this is that you have to complete a self-assessment income tax return and pay Class 2 and Class 4 National Insurance contributions as well (part of which goes towards your state pension fund). Filling out a tax return can feel like a very overwhelming process. It's not, really, if your work isn't too complicated and you're not trying to become a non-dom or something. Becoming Schedule D does have some significant benefits; namely, that you're allowed to offset a certain amount of the expenses you've accrued during the fiscal year against your tax burden. If, like me, the numerical part of your brain doesn't function all that well, what it really means is that as long as you keep your receipts (bravo to Jill for pointing that out above), you can claim things like office, travel and marketing costs as tax deductible. There is also scope to claim back some of, say, the utilities you spent lighting and heating your home office, or part of the cost if you bought a computer for work or a Netflix subscription in order to write a weekly recap of their shows. Please be aware that this is not a bottomless pit of expense-claiming. As you might imagine, there are rules and regulations which are outlined on the government's website. So tread carefully, be honest and stay on top of what you're doing.

The alternative – which is one I employ – is to hire an accountant to do it all for you. It'll cost you and firms charge more for self-employed clients because the tax return takes more time to do and is more complex. But they should ensure you are abiding by the rules while paying an amount to the Inland Revenue which won't bankrupt you annually. To this end, it's imperative you immediately set up a separate bank account – I call mine, drum roll, Tax Account – into which you should siphon a percentage of the money every time you're paid for a freelance job. Different companies do it differently, but often you're paid for a freelance job in full; that is, without any tax being deducted. It will be up to you to pay the income tax on that amount, so make sure you've saved during the year. You don't want to be scrabbling around on some payday loan website come January and July in order to give the government what they demand.

In terms of freelance rates, well, I'd like to tell you that there's a consensus, but that would be wrong. The National Union of Journalists (NUJ) publish an annual freelance fees guide, but it's mostly nonsense. Not because the NUJ are out of touch (they're great), but because in this gig economy it's all about supply and demand. For example, the fee I'm getting for this book, which is essentially a freelance project, comes in significantly under the guidelines for book writing on in the NUJ database. That's not me disparaging my publishers; that's me acknowledging that there are lots of factors at play when it comes to how much you'll be paid. The reality is that rates have decreased significantly over the years. I was one of the first people to write for the BBC Films website back in 1999. At the time, they paid me £100 per review. No more than two years later, the very nice editor wrote to me and told me they were reducing that to £40. Day rates – that is the amount you're paid if you work a shift in a media office for a day – can be anything from £90 to £250 (I've experienced both ends of that spectrum at any one time). One freelance gig involved me being paid in US dollars. Since the office I was hired by was based in Britain, we started out by equating the dollar amount to the pound sterling equivalent. Over the time that I worked there, the pound dropped significantly in value against the dollar. Initially, I carried on being paid the same dollar amount, which was great. But eventually that was renegotiated down so there was equivalency again.

Don't ever be afraid to ask for money, and don't ever be afraid to suggest that you should be offered more, however terrifying that sounds. It's vital that you value your own work, which is also why it's so important that any aspiring journalist pays in some way for their news, by subscribing to something, or doing it by crowdfunding. If you don't think that journalism is worth paying for, then why should anyone pay for yours? That said, be realistic and realise that journalism is unlikely to make you a millionaire, unless you get very lucky. There are areas of large financial reward – a newspaper column or a long-form piece in a US magazine, and now with potential ad revenue sharing on vlogging platforms and companies like Kickstarter or Patreon, it's possible to source your wages directly from your audience. Working in broadcast, particularly television, tends to be more lucrative. If you work as a producer/director on a documentary, you might be looking at, say, £1500 a week or more. If you're really lucky, you might get to ghostwrite a celebrity memoir, which will probably net you 10% or so of their six-figure advance, or maybe Hollywood will option an article you wrote and turn it into a movie (all the more reason to come up with cool ideas). But all this is speculative. Your first job is to get paid for your work. The rest can come later. Just make sure you report it correctly to the HMRC.

Ten top tips – selling as a freelance journalist

1. This is very difficult to do. If you want it, don't give up.
2. Remember that editors are fans of solutions journalism. They need you to answer their questions and difficulties, not pose them new ones.
3. Read the outlet you're pitching to! And not just the most recent issue/page. This also means recognising house style.
4. It's worth being an expert in something. I used to have a student who knew everything there was to know about electro-swing music (nope, still means nothing to me). It may be niche, but it potentially gives you a way in.
5. However, it's also important to know about the mainstream stuff. An editor of mine was once looking for a young journalist to write some film material for them. I pitched a student I knew maintained a movie blog, but turns out she didn't know anything about Star Wars. Having specific knowledge in your chosen area is important, but so is having a broad understanding of what's happening in popular culture generally. There aren't *that* many movie sites which don't cover blockbuster cinema releases.
6. Personal brand is crucial. It's worth reading a few books about the subject so that you're able to exploit yourself and properly understand the public perception of you.
7. Spend a couple of weeks building yourself a good portfolio website. Make it look sexy and cool (as I mentioned earlier, I use Wix, which has nice design elements but requires zero coding skills). It will be any potential employer's first port of call after you've pitched to them.
8. You'll need *a lot* of ideas. Most – 90% unless you're either brilliant or massively flukey – won't get picked up. So you have to have a huge swathe of possible stories ready to go every single day.
9. Be entrepreneurial. Go to industry events; schmooze. I found out where the *Empire* team drank and collared the features editor when he was drunk. It worked.
10. Don't pussyfoot around a pitch, and don't apologise for contacting an editor. If they don't think you believe you deserve to write for them, they won't sign on.

SUZY COX – COMMERCIAL FEATURES EDITOR, *THE GUARDIAN* AND PREVIOUSLY EDITOR, *heat*

What would you say to a person looking to break into your profession right now?

These days, there is zero excuse not to have a portfolio of published work. There are so many ways to get your words out there. Print cuttings alone are not enough – pitch to websites, start a blog or email newsletter, have an Insta account with a USP, contribute to podcasts – then use social to show you know how to amplify the reach of the content you're creating.

Also, yes, social media means it's easier than ever before to contact editors and encourages you to do so conversationally, but if you are introducing yourself for the first time, applying for a job or pitching an idea, think about how you're representing yourself. For example, don't put kisses at the end of an email, do run a spell check and don't ask me a question you can easily find the answer to online or by reading my publication. You want to be a journalist – you won't get far in this game if you demonstrate you can't find out really basic information on your own.

What are the three most important things you need as an editor?

1.   To be able to cut through the hype to work out what the big stories are. With the Internet, streaming services and apps, there's never been more noise out there. Curation is key for *heat's* audience, whether it's telling them which new box set to stream or what's really going on with Posh and Becks. It's my job to edit the information out there for them.

2.   Being a trendspotter – reading *heat* should be like talking to your smartest, most in the know, clever friend. I had to watch a lot of TV, play with a lot of Snapchat filters and catch a lot of Pokémon to research what the hottest new pop culture crazes are.

3.   Listening to your team's input – as an editor, you don't have to know everything and you can't possibly. At *heat*, we had an unbeatable team of pop culture obsessives and unrivalled experts. We were the only magazine to have a dedicated film editor in Charles Gant, and Boyd Hilton is the king of TV: he hosts Sky's Oscar coverage, BBC talent panels … Both are BAFTA judges. They – along with our amazing news and fashion teams – are here because they're the best in their field. It's really important I take their tips and lead.

4.   Oh – and 4. Never think you're the reader. If *heat* had been *Suzy Weekly* it would be full of cats, American teen TV and Kylie. Clearly – while readers want to read about those things (who wouldn't?) – they also love some shows and celebs I'm not always obsessed with. As an editor you need to know your readers inside out. Talk to them on social, see what they're tweeting about your covers and do regular reader research (we have reader pizza nights every few months to get a gauge of what we're doing well and what needs work). Luckily, *heat* readers are really vocal – I took Torso of the Week out for one issue and eight of them emailed me to say I'd ruined their lunch breaks so could I put it back in. I did! Stat.

What do you know now that you wish you'd known when you became a showbiz journalist and then subsequently an editor?

The cliché that the smaller the star, the bigger their ego is – sadly – very often true. Z-listers are frequently more difficult than A-listers. When stars are lovely, you really appreciate it (Joanna Lumley = most gracious, classy lady you can ever meet).

Never take it personally if a PR or an agent has a go at you – it's probably a sign you're doing your job properly and not just writing puff pieces about their client.

By the time you become an editor, you'll spend more of your day at a computer than drinking fizz with cast of TOWIE. The higher up you get, the less you do what you got into it for. But that's okay because new avenues you didn't know existed open.

How do you see the future of your profession and what might a young person need to know moving forward?

People will always want to hear compelling stories told in a credible, clever, interesting and accessible way. What platform those stories are told on might change, but we'll always need unbiased, truthful journalists to tell them.

You have to be flexible and unafraid to learn new things. When I started out, Facebook wasn't even live. Now it's a news source, a way to interact with your readers, amplify your brand, digitally doorstep case studies, broadcast live from your office, find out what your readers think of a star or news event … It's exciting to think what will come next.

Tell us about your favourite moment/s in your job.

For a gossip fiend like me, sitting in conference every morning is a JOY. Getting to see paparazzi pictures first and hearing all the unprintable gossip … The best is when the news team come in with an unbelievable exclusive – like the time they told me they had proof [singer] Cheryl and Liam [Payne] were dating. It sounded totally, totally ridiculous back then – but I trusted them and they were totally right. As a result, we were the first magazine to break it.

When we asked Alan Carr to be *heat*'s first guest editor last year. The special relationship we've nurtured with Alan over the years meant he agreed not just to put his name to it, but [he] put aside a huge chunk of time and [threw] himself into the task. He didn't just oversee the print product but the entire *heat* brand – online, social and even radio.

It was a phenomenal success – the press coverage was worth £416,632 and sales were up 19.2% versus the average. For the first time ever, readers could watch the magazine conference live on Facebook. Shot with three cameras, it was a 60-minute production (Alan only said the word "tit" once) reaching an unprecedented 638,000 *heat* fans.

(Interview with author, 2017)

11

BREAKING INTO THE INDUSTRY

So there we have it. Eleven chapters of a book (including this one; plus, an introduction!) designed to help you become a successful entertainment journalist. Hopefully there are plenty of tips for actually getting into the industry itself scattered throughout the previous however many words – in fact, all the expert interviews contain direct advice to that effect – but I thought to finish, it might be worth focusing more specifically on some things which might help you take the leap from wannabe journalist to real one (hint: mostly it's about convincing yourself that you are and just doing it). To that end, I've created a multipoint plan, which I've titled "Ways to become a successful entertainment journalist". There's a bit of crossover if you've the read the whole of this text, but I hope it's a succinct way of helping you think about and take the next step.

Don't be afraid to start small

Journalism can sometimes be the kind of career to which we attach the same lofty goals as someone in entertainment. In the latter, you're failing unless you've won an Oscar, got a number one single, are the lead on a hit TV show. By the same measure, there can be a perception when you're starting out that you're only successful if you're writing front-page splashes in *The Times*, are editor of *Cosmopolitan* or have the highest-rated podcast on iTunes that has gone viral and made you famous around the world. These are all great things to aspire to, and I hope you achieve them all. But it's important to remember at the beginning that there are a lot of well-respected, contented, solidly remunerated journalists who aren't any of those things and never will be. One of the happiest actors I've ever interviewed was a guy called Perry King. You probably haven't heard of him. He predominantly works on TV, but back in the late 1970s he auditioned to play both Han Solo in the original *Star Wars* and Superman in the 1978 movie. Obviously he didn't get either role. Now, the fact you've never heard of him and that Harrison Ford is one of the most famous stars in Hollywood history would make some think that King lost out, that he missed the big time because he isn't a massive star. Well, King has worked non-stop for 40 years and owns multiple homes. He's also able to walk down the street without someone accosting him for a selfie. There's no failure in that.

Some of you may hit the big time first time out – with a smash-hit YouTube channel or a podcast or on the showbiz desk of a national newspaper. Fantastic. But if you don't, if it takes you a while, if your career is a little peripatetic, don't fret. What I would say is that you should try and have a strong sense of where you would like to be going and do your utmost to push yourself in that direction.

Curate your social

We talked about this in Chapter 6, but I'd like to reiterate it here. If you want to work in music journalism, then make sure your social media channels are full of interesting news and opinions about music. If you want to be a music journalist specialising in country and western, make sure that genre dominates your timelines and is somewhere in your bio. A quick word too about your email address. You know that one iggybeachballhead65@hotmail.com? Well, unless your name is actually Iggy Beachballhead, then change it to something which sounds more professional and includes your name. This is the email address from which you will be pitching to editors, writing to PRs or asking interviewees to give you 20 minutes of their time. If the address that pops up in their inbox sounds lightweight and jokey, they'll think you are too. Among the key skills for any journalist now are being able to write great social headlines and understanding how to sell something on Facebook. Hopefully I've helped you in that regard, but keep looking out for excellent examples of stories or content providers who do this well.

Be the one who goes the extra mile

There will be lots of people who want to do the job that you want to do. Unfortunately, the days of falling into the office of a local paper straight out of school or university are gone. So in order to make yourself more attractive to employers, you need to demonstrate to them that you will pursue something to the nth degree. As I've said earlier, journalism is as much about graft as anything else. Stay that extra few minutes at a premiere, send out another ten emails, try contacting that interviewee again even if they haven't picked up the four times before that. Show that you are willing to go above and beyond. Because if you don't, then someone else will.

"Do you take sugar with that?"

Work experience, or unpaid internships as they now appear to be called (an insidious development in my opinion), are, whether you like it or not, a fundamental part of a journalist's career these days. When I started, you used to pop into an office for a fortnight, shadow some of the staff, write something or witness some filming if you were lucky, spend the week sorting mail if you weren't. Nowadays, companies do often tend to use interns as unpaid labour (there's a whole other book to be written about this and plenty of material which can be found online). Personally, I'm pro work experience, but only for short periods of time. I think it's a good CV builder; it helps you understand what it's like to work in a professional environment. You never really know the buzz of a live newsroom studio until you step into one, trying to avoid the cables and the shouting. You can't get a sense of what it's like to put a weekly magazine to bed until you've experienced the week from initial editorial meeting through to the issue being sent to the printers a few days later.

What you do have to remember is that people are busy. More companies now are setting up proper internships where they ensure someone coming in gets a good experience and is utilised properly. There are lots of places, however, that don't. The key is not to sit there and whinge about it. One of the number one complaints I hear from peers about their 'workies' is that the latter often consider themselves too grand to make the tea. Let me give you one of the best pieces of advice you'll ever get – if you constantly ask to make tea for the staff where you're interning, you'll instantly become one of their favourites and therefore far more likely to be asked back/offered something when the time comes. I'm not saying the secret to making it as a journalist is about being a brew slave. But it demonstrates willingness; it shows that you aren't afraid to get your hands dirty; it shows that you are part of the office. And you know, it's a nice thing to do! I heard a story of one work experience person who walked into the office wearing a T-shirt covered in squares featuring different shades of brown. He'd apparently walk up to each person in the office and ask "which colour?", referring to how milky they wanted their beverage. Now, that's a bit over the top (though here I am recounting it in a journalism textbook so it must have worked in a way), but what I'm saying is don't think you're too good for fetching and carrying. It may be frustrating at first, but it'll pay off, promise.

Know what you're talking about

This can be a difficult one sometimes because there is jargon aplenty in journalism. TV is full of it – when a name appears on the bottom of the screen, it can be called an aston, a super or a lower third, and those are just three that I've heard being used. But the more you can familiarise yourself with this kind of stuff, the more comfortable you'll be when you finally do get into a professional environment during, for instance, a work placement. People screaming about kerning and orphans can be daunting if you don't know what they're talking about. Some of you will be lucky and be, or have been on, practically focused courses that talk about this kind of thing when you have an InDesign masterclass or run a TV gallery. Others may not. If it's the latter, then try and get to grips with some of it by reading other books about journalism or Googling it. That way, when you get an interview for a job at an online outlet, you will be able to talk confidently about UUs (unique users) and ROI (return on investment), which will make you seem like someone who can be inserted straight into that kind of environment.

Lights, camera, action

We've talked at length about the need for multimedia skills, so I won't go over this in too much detail here. Suffice to say, download that Adobe Creative Suite free 30-day trial and practice along with some YouTube tutorials. Buy a cheap gif maker and if you don't know already, teach yourself how to make funny or clever ones. It'll give you an advantage now, but in the future it's likely to be imperative to any young journalist's CV.

Dont forgett – gramar and spelling realy matter, o'kay?

One of the downsides of the squeeze in journalism budgets has been the loss of subeditors; that is, people who check copy before it goes to print/online. I think this is because the rise of online material made owners believe that since you're able to fix any mistakes after publication by changing the back end, subs are expendable. That's a wrong-headed assumption. But there's still a lot less of them, which means that you are going to be responsible for producing clean copy, often very quickly, that stands up to public scrutiny. Some of you will point out the fact there are probably spelling or grammar mistakes somewhere in this book. Congratulations, you win. But for you as someone trying to break into the industry, this is a very easy way to be dismissed by editors and employers who, as I've said before, are longing for people to solve their problems rather than create new ones. Proofread your stuff; don't rely on spellcheck. This is especially true if you're pitching something or sending in a CV – any accuracy errors will result in it being thrown in the bin. That's a very straightforward marker of whether someone is worth hiring or not. I still remember getting screamed at by my boss because a TV actor was said to be starring in *Eastenders* rather than *EastEnders* when his name flashed up on screen during a show I was producing. Bad spelling and punctuation errors are a sure-fire and utterly pointless way of making you seem more amateur than you really are. Do your very best to avoid them.

Added value you

Are you doing something that an employer can't get anywhere else? What makes you indispensable? This doesn't mean you need to be trilingual (although if you are, fantastic), but it does mean trying to think of incremental ways to be 0.5% better than everyone around you. How can you add value to the company you're applying for? Make the answer to that question specific, not just, "I try harder, I'm even more punctual ..." If you can explain why you can, you'll do well.

TOM BUTLER – EDITOR, YAHOO MOVIES UK

What would you say to a person looking to break into your profession right now?

There's no one fixed route into becoming a movie journalist. Everyone I meet seems to have done it differently, but the one thing they have in common is that they've all worked really hard to get to where they are.

Although entertainment can seem fun, alluring and glamorous, I promise you the glitzy side of things is only a tiny fraction of the actual day-to-day job, so if you're in it just to meet movie stars, you're better off going to premieres and getting selfies with the stars on the red carpet. Once you're on the other side, there's no time for fanboy-ism.

Work experience may prove hard to come by, but that shouldn't stop you from writing about movies every day. By maintaining a regular blog, you'll be able to build up a portfolio of work that you can easily share, get instant feedback from your peers and develop your voice.

Make sure you're active and engaged on social media, and try to interact with people and brands you look up to in a meaningful and positive way. You're more likely to get your foot in the door and hear about opportunities if you can be seen and heard in places where journalists like to interact, such as Twitter.

What are the three most important things you need as a movie journalist?

1. An encyclopaedic knowledge of movies and cinema history, and not just the mainstream stuff. You need to be on top of the latest industry developments and movie trends and have a working knowledge of how films are made and distributed.
2. It also helps to nurture your niche interests as editors like myself are inundated with blockbuster experts. If you like horror, become a horror expert; if you're passionate about British cinema, become an advocate for British cinema; if Transformers are your thing, become the go-to guy for Transformers.
3. You need to have a good sense of what works for your audience and be able to adapt to their demand. Every media outlet exists to cater for its specific audience; if you can't tune in to their needs and produce content they want, then you won't last long. This will come through a mixture of research, analytics, and trial and error, but it's the willingness and ability to experiment with form and content that will get you ahead. There's so much churn within the daily news grind, you need to be able to conjure up new and interesting angles with the blink of an eye.
4. In the modern digital era I think it's essential for journalists to have complete mastery of all aspects of multimedia. Being able to write good copy simply isn't enough. You must also be able to picture edit, write video

scripts, edit audio, shoot video, create graphics, as well as live presenting, interviewing, chasing down stories, and social media. The more strings you have to your bow, the more employable you become.

What do you know now that you wish you'd known when you became a film journalist?

It probably won't make me rich. Seriously, unless you're in one of the very few top-tier jobs, being a movie journalist should be your passion, as it's probably not going to make you a millionaire.

Also, the higher up you go, the less time there is for the fun stuff. There are some amazing perks to this job, but it's also very high pressured, and so the further you progress, the more you have to delegate the fun stuff to someone else.

How do you see the future of your profession and what might a young person need to know moving forward?

People will always want movies content, but print is currently at a dead end. I'd also say that traditional online reporting will need to develop to stay ahead of the game too. Younger people consume media in different ways and we need to adapt, so stay ahead of the trends. Innovate; don't imitate.

What's the best thing about your job?

Free screenings, without a shadow of a doubt. The occasional travel is nice and meeting movie stars on a daily basis will always make for a fun conversation with your family or friends down the pub.

Tell us about your favourite moment/s in the job?

Standing in Avengers Towers watching Robert Downey Jr, Chris Evans, Scarlett Johansson, Chris Hemsworth, Mark Ruffalo, Jeremy Renner, Don Cheadle and Anthony Mackie perform scenes as the Avengers on the set of *Age of Ultron*. Also interviewing Tony Stark and Thor, in costume, in Robert Downey Jr's personal trailer park at Pinewood.

Fulfilling a lifelong dream of interviewing the cast of a Star Wars film when doing the press junket for *Rogue One*.

Interviewing Chris Nolan and Michael Caine – plus Jessica Chastain, Anne Hathaway and Matthew McConaughey – for *Interstellar*. But mainly Michael Caine. Anyone who says never meet your heroes has never met Michael Caine.

(Interview with author, 2017)

Who played Jar Jar Binks?

Lots of people want to write for film magazines. Lots of people want to write about fashion and music and theatre. It sounds a bit ridiculous out of context, but when I worked premieres, I was known as the "Ben-cyclopaedia" (please note that I didn't come up with that myself!). Every person walking down that red carpet, I knew who they were. I knew what TV show they'd starred in and who they'd starred with, and that meant I was able to come up with an interesting and relevant question for them. Often people seem to want to be an entertainment journalist because they think it's cool. That it's more interesting than, say, business journalism. They'll get to meet famous people and maybe go to fancy places. As lots of the expert interviews in this book will tell you – you've got to soak yourself in your field. You've got to be a soap opera nerd. Or you've got to know everything there is about grime. Or you need to be able to answer questions about every corner of the expanded Marvel universe. This ties in with the above point – your special brain is something you bring to the table.

Tony Robbins' human needs

Tony Robbins is this really tall, big-toothed American self-help guru who was huge in the 1990s. But while he helped CEOs make even more money and cropped up in movies like *Men in Black*, his interest in marketing and brand led him to come up with six human needs which he says are at the core of every human decision and desire. Branding experts have since appropriated these for marketing. And in that way, I'm doing the same thing in terms of how you can market yourself to employers. If you can fulfil at least three of these six needs for someone who might hire you, you'll be in with a good shout.

- *Certainty* – this is about comfort and it ties back to 'solutions journalism', which I discussed earlier. In other words, are you a safe pair of hands?
- *Uncertainty* – it's about variety, surprise. Can you be surprising, in a good way, to an employer?
- *Significance* – this is about you … *and* them. Can you make the employer feel important or special? Feel like they're the only ones doing what they're doing so brilliantly? Really this is about flattery. Conversely, can you demonstrate to them that by hiring you, they're getting something unique? Something that everyone else wants and is desperate to get their hands on?
- *Connection* – people forget that you'll spend more time with your work colleagues than you do your own family. When Robert Downey Jr. was at the height of his drug addiction, people still hired him because they liked being around him, even if his life was messy. The same goes for employers – do they want to hang out in the office with you? Can they imagine you at a work away day? Can they see you as a complementary part of the team?
- *Growth* – you need to demonstrate that by hiring you, their company is getting bigger and better. Robbins said that if you're not growing, you're dying. So

that means you always thinking of ways to grow yourself too (new skills, new ideas, innovation).

- *Contribution* – Robbins wrote on Entrepreneur.com that "sharing enhances everything you experience". Taking this literally, you can help a potential hirer share what they've created with the world. You must convince employers how you can help their message and vision get into the world and make it better.

Entrepreneurialism

You may not have the swagger of Tony Robbins, but you will need to think entrepreneurially to succeed. That may be by actually creating your own media space or product, creating a Kickstarter page, or trying to fund your idea as a non-profit or through venture capitalists. But on a more personal level, you need to think clinically about how to push your brand and what you're trying to achieve in your content creation if you want to turn it into something professional and moneymaking. So is your website merely a portfolio, or is it trying to move the news agenda? PerezHilton began as a blog, but he was always trying to tell new stories (whether you agree with how he did it or not). Of course, if you do something like that well, then it automatically transforms into a portfolio for yourself. Have conversations that could lead to business opportunities. Put yourself in amongst people who might be in a position to help you, like at an industry event. Become part of the conversation and put yourself at the centre of the community you want to engage. To further the business metaphor, glean data from your contacts through their social feeds (no, I'm not talking about stalking – I'm talking about being up to date with what's going on in their world) and think about how they might discover you. Set yourself goals – create milestones for when you want to be doing something. Treat yourself, in a way, like a product. Why does the entertainment journalism world need *you*? And find out what employers need through analysis and market research.

This year's birthday present – a media subscription

One of the prevailing things I hear from my students is that they want to work in the field of entertainment journalism, but they don't actually buy any magazines or newspapers or even watch much TV. They just look at what's on Facebook and watch some YouTube channels. Now, social media will disseminate a great deal of content, and you might well want to become an expert on vloggers and that's fine. But to succeed, you've absolutely got to know the industry and its different facets. So for your birthday this year, how about skipping the video games or the shopping voucher and asking your family for a subscription to a magazine you love that will help you burrow deeper into the world of entertainment? Or to something like Blendle, an app which allows you to make micropayments to read brands like *Vanity Fair*? Or perhaps a daily delivery of the *Guardian* or *The Sun*?

Whatever you choose, read it cover to cover and then think about how they did it and why they did it.

Why not you? Have faith

When I went for an interview to do a postgraduate journalism degree at quite a prestigious institution, I was asked who I wanted to write for. I told them I would love to be a film journalist and I was hoping to write for *Empire*. The interviewer smiled and explained that it was very difficult to get a job at a place like that, because so many people want to do it. I smiled back. By the time I arrived there seven months later, I was freelancing for *Empire*. My thought was always, "Well, it doesn't get written by a robot. People work there, so why shouldn't it be me?"

Most journalists are not geniuses. Getting a job at a magazine or newspaper or production company is highly coveted, sure, but it's not like you're trying to become prime minister – more than a handful of people get to do it. Why shouldn't it be you? If you're confident and keen and have done the research and you're prepared to work hard and, yes, you have a bit of luck, then there is absolutely not reason why you can't get the job you want. It'll require passion and dedication and there'll be some difficult times, but magazines need to be designed and written, Twitter channels need to be updated, programmes need to be filmed and presented. These days, content is king. The industry may have contracted in many ways, but it's also opened up countless different opportunities. And we don't even know what's going to happen in the future, what skills might be needed, how television channels are going to function or what new social platforms will be created. They're going to need people to make it, to run it, to be a part of it. Driven, excited, talented, innovative, thoughtful people.

Why not you?

Ten top tips – breaking into the entertainment journalism industry

1. Journalists are just people – often very geeky people. Don't be scared of them. Don't think they are cooler than you. I used to and I regretted it. You deserve to be there.
2. Marketers will tell you that you can't fake trust. Make any potential employer trust you with your insights, attitude and statements. It's about being consistent and clear.
3. Let's not sugarcoat this – journalism is a hugely difficult industry to break into. But someone's got to do it, so why couldn't it be you? Don't give up.
4. Think about how you can add value. How are you indispensable to someone? Are you?
5. Flattery will get you everywhere. Journalists are rarely told when they've done something brilliant. So find something you think is fantastic, work out who created it and then tweet them about it, asking if you could meet up for a coffee. Then stroke their ego some more.

6. Figure out where the people from your dream magazine/newspaper/website like to socialise after work. Relaxed editors are more suggestible.

7. Don't be afraid to write for free, but don't do it for too long.

8. Don't be afraid to work for free, but see number 7 about the length of time.

9. If you do work experience (they're called internships now, but should only really be called that if you're doing it while you're at university and are getting academic credit for it), make tea. It's not demeaning; it's a great way to meet and find out about the staff.

10. When you've made it, always be prepared to help the next young person make it too. No one ever succeeds by themselves – they need someone higher up the totem pole to say yes and let them into the club. Don't ever forget that.

ORLANDO PARFITT – ONLINE EDITOR, *SCREEN INTERNATIONAL*

What would you say to a person looking to break into your profession right now?

It's hard. Lots of media companies are shrinking and most aren't making money. Nonetheless it's still an exciting industry to be a part of, and its rapidly changing nature means there are more opportunities than ever for young journalists if they understand the latest social platforms.

What are the three most important things you need as an online journalist?

1. The basics: meaning writing clean, error-free copy that is properly fact-checked and reads well. Amazing how many young (and not so young) journalists forget this.

2. You should be able to do most of the following: build engaging Facebook and Twitter posts and maintain professional social media pages; basic video editing, including uploading to YouTube; basic Photoshop; know how to make a gif; be able to write snappy headlines; understand basic online copyright law. I do almost all of these things on a daily basis.

3. Understanding data. So much online journalism is now data-driven. Not just page views, but what kind of page views – social referrals, SEO traffic. Journalists need to be able to understand this kind of data and let it inform their work.

What do you know now that you wish you'd known when you became an online entertainment journalist?

That knowing people and networking is very important. Every job I've ever got has been through knowing someone. Also, this is a random and sometimes harsh industry. At some point you will lose your job because of cutbacks, etc. It happened to me but it ended up being a blessing in disguise.

As an online editor, what are you looking for from any young journalist who's approaching/pitching you?

First of all, evidence they can do the basics (see above). Even if they haven't had anything published, examples of articles they have written are essential. I need to see they can write.

Secondly, I want pitches that can help me. Look at the site you are pitching for. What kind of content do they run? Has a similar article idea you're pitching actually been on that site? If so, scrap it and come up with something original. I've been pitched a lot of generic ideas and I will usually ignore them, but if I'm pitched something interesting, even if the author doesn't have much experience, then I might commission them.

How do you see the future of your profession and what might a young person need to know moving forward?

As I said before, it's a volatile industry; there are constant cutbacks and lots of people constantly losing their jobs. This will keep happening as newspaper/magazine circulation continues to decline and digital publishers continue to struggle with monetisation.

On the other hand, there is more content being published than ever and more places to get it published. The industry is now much more fluid – who could've predicted ten years ago that Buzzfeed would be one of the dominant media brands in the world? Or that a traditional red top like The Sun would've hired an entire team of people to produce Snapchat videos? Being open to change and learning new things constantly will be a vital part of being a journalist – alongside the basics.

What's the best thing about your job?

I'm very lucky that I get to report on an industry I love and am passionate about (the film business). I also get to talk to very interesting people. In the past month I've interviewed the head of BAFTA, the creator of The Crown and the leading actor in the latest Star Wars film.

What are some of your favourite moments from your career?

I interviewed Sir Ian McKellen (a personal hero) on the set of The Hobbit. I got this opportunity because I was an experienced film journalist. This was a niche I'd carved for myself over ten years – from being the film critic of my student paper to doing unpaid work experience at a film mag. Having an area of expertise, be it film, travel, fashion or even fly fishing is really helpful.

I got an exclusive story that went viral and ended up on the front cover of several trade mags. The story came from three different filmed interviews that I cut together into one video. The learning point is, firstly, don't be afraid to ask tough questions – that's how I got my scoop. Also the video editing – something I'm not trained in but am self-taught enough to do the basics, and it really made the story work. Having to teach yourself new skills constantly is vital in this job. Being an employable online journalist is not just about being a decent writer.

(Interview with author, 2017)

BIBLIOGRAPHY

Print

Addison, A. (2017). *Mail Men: The Unauthorized Story of the* Daily Mail – *The Paper that Divided and Conquered Britain*. London: Atlantic Books.

Barnes, R.D. (2010). *Outrageous Invasions: Celebrities' Private Lives, Media, and the Law*. Oxford: Oxford University Press.

Bernstein, S. (2006). *Mr Confidential: The Man, His Magazine and the Movieland Massacre that Changed Hollywood Forever*. London: Walford Press.

Best, K.N. (2017). *The History of Fashion Journalism*. London: Bloomsbury Academic.

Brantley, W., ed., (1996). *Conversations with Pauline Kael*. Jackson, MS: University Press of Mississippi.

Bull, R., ed., (2014). *Investigative Interviewing*. New York: Springer.

Bussmann, J. (2009). *The Worst Date Ever*. London: Macmillan.

Conboy, M. (2001). *The Press and Popular Culture*. London: Sage.

Conboy, M. (2005). *Tabloid Britain*. New York: Routledge.

Conboy, M. (2011). *Journalism in Britain: A Historical Introduction*. London: Sage.

Conboy, M. and Steel, J., eds. (2014). *The Routledge Companion to British Media History*. London: Routledge.

Dahlgren, P. and Sparks, C., eds. (1992). *Journalism and Popular Culture*. London: SAGE.

Daly, C.B. (2012). *Covering America: A Narrative History of a Nation's Journalism*. Amherst, MA: University of Massachusetts Press.

Epstein, E.J. (2014). *EXTRA: The Inventions of Journalism*. EJE Publications Ltd.

Evans, R. (1994). *The Kid Stays in the Picture*. New York: Hyperion Books.

Falk, Q. (2011). Critical Mass: The Depreciating Value of Film Criticism. *Moviescope* [author's manuscript].

Forrest, H. (2013). *Confessions of a Showbiz Reporter*. London: The Friday Project Limited.

Franklin, B. (1955). *An Apology for Printers*. New York: Book Craftsmen Associates, Inc.

Frith, M. (2008). *The Celeb Diaries: The Sensational Inside Story of the Celebrity Decade*. London: Ebury Press.

Horrie, C. (2003). *Tabloid Nation: The Birth of the* Daily Mirror *to the Death of the Tabloid*. London: André Deutsch.

Inge, M.T., ed. (1987). *Truman Capote: Conversations*. Jackson, MS: University Press of Mississippi.

Kauffmann, S. (1966). *A World on Film*. New York: Harper & Row.

Keeble, R. (2008). *Ethics for Journalists*. London: Routledge.

Kermode, M. (2011). *The Good, The Bad and the Multiplex*. London: Random House.

Knight, M. and Cook, C. (2013). *Social Media for Journalists: Principles and Practice*. London: Sage.

Leveson, B. (2012). *An Inquiry into the Culture, Practices and Ethics of the Press: Executive Summary And Recommendations*. London: House of Commons.

Marshall, P. (2005). Celebrity and Journalism. In: S. Allan, ed., *Journalism: Critical Issues*. Maidenhead: Open University Press, pp. 19–28.

Marshall, S. (2010). *Tabloid Girl*. London: Sphere.

McKay, J. (2013). *The Magazines Handbook*. 3rd ed. Oxford: Routledge.

Norman, B. (2002). *And Why Not? Memoirs of a Film Lover*. London: Simon & Schuster.

Quinn, F. (2013). *Law for Journalists*. 4th ed. Harlow: Pearson.

Silverman, C. (2012). A New Age of Truth. *Nieman Reports*, 66(2).

Silvester, C. (1993). *The Penguin Book of Interviews*. London: Viking.

Slide, A. (2010). *Inside the Hollywood Fan Magazine: A History of Star Makers, Fabricators, and Gossip Mongers*. Jackson, MS: University Press of Mississippi.

Thomson, D. (2016). *Television: A Biography*. New York: Thames and Hudson Ltd.

Vanderhallen, M. and Vervaeke, G. (2014). Between Investigator and Suspect: The Role of the Working Alliance in Investigative Interviewing. In: R. Bull, ed., *Investigative Interviewing*. New York: Springer, pp. 63–90.

Wenner, J. (2017). *50 Years of Rolling Stone: The Music, Politics and People that Changed Our Culture*. New York: Abrams Books.

Online

Adewunmi, B. (2013). Mark Kermode: The next generation of film critics will come from the Internet. *New Statesman*, 14 February. Available at: www.newstatesman.com/culture/2013/02/mark-kermode-next-generation-film-critics-will-come-internet [Accessed 21 Jan. 2017].

Anthony, S. (2016). Enter the secret world of social media managers. *Social Media Week*. Available at: https://socialmediaweek.org/blog/2016/10/enter-secret-world-social-media-managers/ [Accessed 2 May 2017].

BBC (2016). First official UK press regulator, Impress, approved. *BBC News*, 25 October. www.bbc.co.uk/news/uk-37758497 [Accessed 21 Nov. 2017].

Borkowski, M. (2008). A changing world puts public relations in a spin. *The Independent*. Available at: www.independent.co.uk/news/media/a-changing-world-puts-public-relations-in-a-spin-783490.html [Accessed 21 Nov. 2017].

Borkowski, M. (2014). Journalist bites PR: Never explain, never complain. *Mark My Words*, 24 February. Available at: www.markborkowski.co.uk/journalist-bites-pr-never-explain-never-complain/ [Accessed 21 Nov. 2017].

Borkowski, M. (2016). A PR's take on why so many journalists think PRs are not up to the job. *The Drum*, 2 September. Available at: www.thedrum.com/opinion/2016/09/02/prs-take-why-so-many-journalists-think-prs-are-not-job [Accessed 21 Nov. 2017].

Chicago Tribune (1991). Young is better than old. *Chicago Tribune*, 7 October. Available at: http://articles.chicagotribune.com/1991-10-07/news/9103310817_1_country-music-awards-show-vince-gill-elizabeth-taylor [Accessed 21 Sep. 2017].

Contact Law (n.d.). Privacy law. Available at: www.contactlaw.co.uk/49-nolink-uk/areas-of-law/disputes/information-and-privacy-law/729-privacy-law.html [Accessed 21 Nov. 2017].

Defamation Act 2013, Chapter 26. Available at: www.legislation.gov.uk/ukpga/2013/26/section/1/enacted [Accessed 21 Nov. 2017].

Diamond, E. (1985). Celebrating celebrity. *New York Magazine*, 13 May. Available at: https://books.google.co.uk/books?id=ysUBAAAAMBAJ&pg=PA22&lpg=PA22&dq=jann+wenner+call+it+what+you+want+gossip+journalism&source=bl&ots=1_xZFASrtk&sig=YsPRtpxIWW7Oiz0JmARuzEjrT2k&hl=en&sa=X&ved=0ahUKEwjf5Yq20LTWAhVLKsAKHfUoCMwQ6AEINzAG#v=onepage&q=jann%20wenner%20call%20it%20what%20you%20want%20gossip%20journalism&f=false [Accessed 21 Sep. 2017].

Elsworth, C. (2005). Sony ordered to pay $1.5m for film-goer hoax. *The Telegraph*, 5 August. Available at: www.telegraph.co.uk/news/worldnews/northamerica/usa/1495591/Sony-ordered-to-pay-1.5m-for-film-goer-hoax.html [Accessed 16 May 2017].

Hagan, J. and Marr, M. (2006). Caught in the Act! *The Wall Street Journal*, March 4. Available at: www.wsj.com/articles/SB114143524125389337 [Accessed 16 May 2017].

Kirkman, J. (2015). Hot tips on how to interview a comedian. *Jen Kirkman Comedian*, 31 October. Available at: www.jenkirkman.com/jens-blog/definitive-guide-of-how-not-to-interview [Accessed 21 Nov. 2017].

Marshall, S. (2011). Witness statement for the Leveson Inquiry. Available at: http://webarchive.nationalarchives.gov.uk/20140122145147/http:/www.levesoninquiry.org.uk/wp-content/uploads/2011/12/Witness-Statement-of-Sharron-Marshall.pdf [Accessed 21 Nov. 2017].

Powers, J. (2002). Two or three things I know about celebrity journalism. A presentation to the Celebrity, Politics & Public Life faculty seminar, 22 September. Available at: https://learcenter.org/pdf/powers_notes.pdf [Accessed 21 Nov. 2017].

Practical Law (n.d.). Privacy in UK (England and Wales): Overview. Available at: https://uk.practicallaw.thomsonreuters.com/3-525-6372?__lrTS=20170513154731949&transitionType=Default&contextData=(sc.Default)&firstPage=true&bhcp=1 [Accessed 21 Nov. 2017].

Romenesko, J. (2003). Bastone: Most entertainment writers are too cozy with flacks. *Poynter*, 25 September. Available at: www.poynter.org/news/bastone-most-entertainment-writers-are-too-cozy-flacks [Accessed 21 Sep. 2017].

Silver, J. (2006). Gawk, don't talk. [Interview with Nick Denton.], *The Guardian*, 11 December. Available at: www.theguardian.com/technology/2006/dec/11/news.mondaymediasection [Accessed 21 Sep. 2017].

Society of Professional Journalists (2017). SPJ Code of Ethics. Available at: www.spj.org/ethicscode.asp [Accessed 21 Sep. 2017].

Stosuy, B. (2008). Lily Allen and Perez Hilton fight over Katy Perry. *Stereogum*. Available at: www.stereogum.com/10411/lily_allen_takes_on_perez_hilton_makes_creepy_use/wheres-the-beef/ [Accessed 21 Sep. 2017].

UK Parliament (n.d.). Summary of the Defamation Act 2013. Available at: https://services.parliament.uk/bills/2012-13/defamation.html [Accessed 21 Nov. 2017].

Wikipedia (2017). David Manning (fictitious writer). Available at: https://en.wikipedia.org/wiki/David_Manning_(fictitious_writer) [Accessed on 16 May 2017].

Young, K. (2006). Living under the paparazzi's gaze. *BBC News*, 29 July. Available at: http://news.bbc.co.uk/1/hi/entertainment/5224284.stm [Accessed 21 Sep. 2017].

Zulkey, C. (2006). The Mario "Perez Hilton" Lavandeira Jr. Interview. *Zulkey.com*. Available at: http://zulkey.com/2006/11/111006.shtml#.WcLXzneGMfM [Accessed 21 Sep. 2017].

INDEX